YEAR IN THE LIFE OF CHRIST SERIES

3

The Preaching of Jesus

Mark Moore & Jon Weece

International Standard Book Number 0-89900-849-6

TABLE
OF
CONTENTS

4

WHAT A PREACHER!

The guards sent to arrest Jesus returned empty handed. Their superiors in the Sanhedrin berated their failure, "Why didn't you bring him in?" Their defense was simple, "No one ever spoke the way this man does" (John 7:46). It was almost as if Jesus' words created some invisible, impenetrable force field. Some six months later this same Sanhedrin tried their hand at trapping Jesus through a verbal duel. It was right out in the open temple courts, giving the Pharisees home field advantage. They desperately wanted to trap, convict, and kill Jesus. Yet the Bible records they couldn't. Why? "Because all the people hung on his words" (Luke 19:48). At one point Jesus preached a sermon to thronging thousands in the synagogue at Capernaum. It was so offensive that nearly everyone walked away disillusioned. In fact, as the sun set, there were only twelve left at the Master's side. He asked, almost by way of invitation, "Do you want to leave too?" Peter replied, "Lord, to whom shall we go? You have the words of eternal life" (John 6:68).

It's almost unfair to put the word "preaching" in the title of any book about Jesus. Oh sure, that's what Jesus did—he *preached*. But too often that word conjures up some droning monologue on a sleepy Sunday morning. Jesus' sermons weren't received on the backs of stiff wooden pews but in the throes of gritty peasant life. They were filled with captivating stories that bit you in the backside as you walked away. They were peppered with biting sarcasm, impossible demands, and fiery condemnation of religious hypocrites. They turned the social economy on its head with such strange declarations as "the first will be last," "hate your father and mother," and "sell all your possessions." What makes it worse is that Jesus wasn't kidding.

It is no small wonder that people were amazed at his teaching. In fact, the Gospel of Mark records three instances where people were amazed at Jesus' miracles, but seven times it says they were amazed at his words. The preaching of Jesus is simply astounding. In saying that, we are not suggesting it is like a sideshow curiosity. It is not amazing because it is interesting and fun but because it is exacting. Jesus' words have a way of getting on our insides, discomforting our thoughts, and revealing every bit of smug religious self-satisfaction we dare to hold up to shield the relentless onslaught of his words.

Please note: the preaching of Jesus can only be comfortable to those who sleep through it. His ideas are revolutionary; his response to challenges no less than genius. His demands are relentless and his vision is laser sharp. We often come to Jesus' sermons with an exegetical scalpel in hand, ready to respectfully dissect these dormant texts, only to find out they're still alive. They rise from the table, swipe the scalpel from our hands, and proceed to do a spiritual heart transplant with no anesthesia. Jesus' words have a way of getting in your face, and his parables sneak up from behind. His thoughts are too high for us, yet it is imperative that they are the foundation upon which we build our house. For when the storm comes, the words of Jesus are the only secure footings.

The Preaching of Jesus

THE MAGNA CARTA OF THE KINGDOM— PART 1

> There can be no Kingdom of God in the world without the Kingdom of God in our hearts.
> —Albert Schweitzer
>
> What God expects us to attempt, He also enables us to achieve.
> —Stephen Olford

Text: Matthew 5:1–7:29   **Memory:** Matthew 5:20

Strange People   In the "Letter to Diognetus," which dates back to the second century, an anonymous writer describes a strange people who are in the world, but not of the world:

> Christians are not differentiated from other people by country, language, or customs; you see, they do not live in cities of their own, or speak some strange dialect. . . . They live in both Greek and foreign cities, wherever chance has put them. They follow local customs in clothing, food, and the other aspects of life. But at the same time, they demonstrate to us the unusual form of their own citizenship. They live in their own native lands, but as aliens . . . every foreign country is to them as their native country, and every native land as a foreign country. They marry and have children just like everyone else, but they do not kill unwanted

8

babies. They offer a shared table, but not a shared bed. They are passing their days on earth, but are citizens of heaven. They obey the appointed laws and go beyond the laws in their own lives. They love everyone, but are persecuted by all. They are put to death and gain life. They are poor and yet make many rich. They are dishonored and yet gain glory through dishonor. Their names are blackened, and yet they are cleared. They are mocked and bless in return. They are treated outrageously and behave respectfully to others. When they do good, they are punished as evildoers; when punished, they rejoice as if being given new life. They are attacked by Jews as aliens and are persecuted by Greeks; yet those who hate them cannot give any reason for their hostility.

Nearly 2,000 years ago, that writer captured in words, what he was witnessing first hand. And that, my friends, is the people of God living out the Sermon on the Mount.

Overview of the Text

The Sermon on the Mount is arguably the greatest sermon ever preached. Without question it is the most quoted. And why not? It contains the beatitudes, "Turn the other cheek," the Lord's Prayer, "Do not judge. . . ." the golden rule, and that great children's song about the wise man building his house upon the rock. Obviously we can't do justice in such a short space to such a massive discourse. We'll not even try to plumb its depths. What we will attempt, however, is to trace its contours. When its silhouette comes into view, what we see is the kingdom—the rules for the reign of God in our lives. These words are a rock upon which we can build a church, a foundation for a life of faith. Be careful, however, for they are viciously demanding and relentless in their probing of your interior. If you're not careful, they will turn you inside out.

- Take time to read the entire sermon out loud. It will take about 18 minutes. As you do, circle verses that you find particularly meaningful. Put a question mark by statements that you find perplexing. After this exercise, share with the group your questions just over chapter 5 and tell the others why you find your circled verses so significant.
- What are some of the key themes of the sermon?
- How do you think you would have responded to the sermon the very first time you heard it?

Meaning of the Text

If this sermon is a Magna Carta of the kingdom, then what sort of "rules" does it establish? What sort of life does it demand? The answer is both complex and controversial, but there are some rules that clearly surface.

Rule #1: *The kingdom turns the world on its head.* It starts with the beatitudes. They are eight simple statements that radically realign the priorities of kingdom people. The world considers rich people fortunate, likewise those who laugh a lot, have power, comfort, and security. "On the contrary," Jesus says, "They are truly blessed by God who are spiritually bankrupt, mourning in repentance, meek, starving for God," etc. It is as if Jesus divides his audience into two groups. On one side are those who "have it all." They are sure to be key players in Jesus' soon-coming kingdom. On the other side are the riffraff, those which the Jewish leaders called *Am-ha-aretz* (literally "the people of the earth"). These "hoi polloi" are the poor, the sick, the disenfranchised . . . in short the "sinners." They are sure they could never lead out in Christ's kingdom. In a surprising twist, however, Jesus congratulates them for being central to his program. Before the sermon is up and running, he turns the totem pole of priorities upside down. The in are out and the up are down.

How is that fair? How does that make sense? Well, to the world it doesn't—not even to the religious world. But the kingdom is Christ-centered and the poor well know their need for Jesus. The single parent, the widow, the child, the drug addict, they all realize they have no hope in this world to make it on their own. Their only recourse is to turn to God and plead for help. He answers them. The rich, on the other hand, hold onto the glimmer of hope in their own prowess. They have just enough intelligence, power, or savvy to sustain the myth in their own minds that they can be worthy of God. It is this illusion of self-sufficiency that will damn good people to hell. So this kingdom of Christ is an upside-down kingdom that makes no sense to the economy of this society.

Rule #2: *This kingdom demands a rigorous internal righteousness.* In Matthew 5:20, Jesus says, "I tell you that unless your righteousness surpasses that of the Pharisees and the teachers of the law, you will certainly not enter the kingdom of heaven." Now how are we going to work that? These guys fasted twice a week, prayed three times a day, and tithed down to their garden herbs. Is it realistic that our righteous acts will exceed theirs? Honestly, no. Fortunately, that is not what Jesus requires. What he is asking for is not broader righteousness, but deeper righteousness. He's not asking us for more deeds, but purer motives; not a bigger religion, but a deeper relationship. As Thomas Holdcroft put it, "God isn't so concerned with delivering us out of the mess we're in as He is in seeing us grow out of the mess we are."

After making this mind-blowing statement in verse 20, Jesus illustrates it with six specific examples from the Mosaic code. Moses made legal declarations about certain behaviors, and Jesus used each of these to plumb the depths of our hearts. In other words, Jesus says, "I know that your external morality is impeccable, but what does your heart look like?" Watch:

Mosaic Code (and its oral interpretation)	Jesus' Extrapolation	Permissions Restricted; Commands Extended
Don't murder (21-26)	Don't harbor vengeful anger	Extended
Don't commit adultery (27-30)	Don't lust	Extended
Divorce with a certificate (31-32)	Divorce only for adultery	Restricted
Don't break an oath (33-37)	Be completely honest	Extended
Retaliate only with equality (38-42)	Don't retaliate at all. In fact, do good to your enemies.	Restricted
Love your neighbors (43-48)	Love everyone	Extended

This third column of the chart is quite interesting. Whenever the Pharisees encountered a command in the OT, they tended to restrict its demands, they minimized the law to the actual act itself—murder was killing, breaking an oath only dealt with formal and official promises, etc. Jesus, on the other hand, extended commands from the hands to the heart. It wasn't enough to abstain from murder; the root of bitterness had to be eradicated from the heart. It wasn't enough to keep out of a harlot's embrace; one had to eradicate the lustful look that leads to adultery. And on it goes.

When Pharisees encountered promises, on the other hand, they extended them. If one could divorce legally with a certificate, they could divorce almost whimsically (which was as much a problem then as it is today). Or again, if one could retaliate, they would press their victims to the extent of the law. Along comes Jesus. He virtually wipes out every extension, exclusion, addendum, and small print. He simply says, "Do to others what you would have them do to you." He takes away the legalistic rules. He wipes out the pettiness of law keeping and gets at the heart of the issue, which is the heart.

This is overpowering. Up to now the Mosaic Law had been subject to extended debate. Each rabbi added his voice into the ongoing vituperative argument about the meaning of each law. Jesus, with uncanny clarity, reduces all arguments

The Magna Carta of the Kingdom—Part 1

by simplifying God's expectations. Rather than talking about behavior, he talked about motive. Where the heart is pure the hands will be as well. If the hands alone are pure, there is no guarantee the heart will follow.

What is so curious is that Jesus simplified the law, yet made it much more difficult to keep. I had enough trouble loving my friends . . . now I have to serve my enemies! It was hard enough not to break an oath, but to never be dishonest! Yikes! It's difficult enough being sexually pure, but to bridle our thoughts is daunting! Yet if we are to be part of Jesus' kingdom, these are not mere suggestions, these are laws. Jesus said earlier, if you break one of the least of these commands, you will be called least in the kingdom.

> "While serving as a missionary in Laos," tells John Hess-Yoder, "I discovered an illustration of the kingdom of God. Before the colonialists imposed national boundaries, the kings of Laos and Vietnam reached an agreement on taxation in the border areas. Those who ate short-grain rice, built their houses on stilts, and decorated them with Indian-style serpents were considered Laotians. On the other hand, those who ate long-grain rice, built their houses on the ground, and decorated them with Chinese-style dragons were considered Vietnamese. The exact location of a person's home was not what determined his or her nationality. Instead, each person belonged to the kingdom whose cultural values he or she exhibited."[1]

So it is with us: we live in the world, but as part of God's kingdom, we are to live according to his kingdom's standards and values. Further, we must be vigilant to clarify a couple of things here. On the one hand, we are not suggesting that our salvation depends on keeping these laws of the kingdom. We are saved by Jesus' atoning death, no question, no discussion. On the other hand, we must avoid the impression that Jesus' rule has no law. It does and he is it! He has shown us here what his expectations are and he modeled them for us by example. Let's not naively think that grace makes no demands. Our righteousness must reflect the majesty of our king.

Practicing the Preaching of Jesus

Take three statements from chapter 5. Write each one on a 3″×5″ card and place one in your car, one in a prominent place where you work, and one on your bathroom mirror. Simply let the Holy Spirit deal with you through these.

2 THE MAGNA CARTA OF THE KINGDOM— PART 2

2 2

> It is difficult to make a man miserable while he feels worthy of himself and claims kindred to the great God who made him.
> —Abraham Lincoln

> True love comes quietly, without banners or flashing lights. If you hear bells, get your ears checked.
> —Erich Segal

Text: Matthew 6:1–7:29   **Memory:** Matthew 6:33 & 7:12

Lovable Mary Ann Bird grew up knowing she was different and she hated it. She was born with a cleft palate and when she started school, her classmates made it abundantly clear to her how she looked to others: a little girl with a misshapen lip, crooked nose, lopsided teeth, and garbled speech.

When classmates asked, "What happened to your lip?" She'd tell them she'd fallen and cut it on a piece of glass. Somehow it seemed more acceptable to have suffered an accident than to have been born different. She was convinced that no one outside of her family could love her.

There was, however, a teacher in the second grade that everyone adored: Mrs. Leonard. She was a short, happy, sparkling kind of lady.

Annually Mrs. Leonard administered a hearing test in

her classroom. The routine was easy to understand. Each student was asked to stand outside the classroom, cover one ear with a hand and place the other ear against the door. Then, Mrs. Leonard would whisper something from the other side and the student would have to repeat it back. She said things like, "The sky is blue." Mary Ann took her turn, doing everything she had been instructed to do, and she waited to hear a similar phrase. Instead, she heard words that were rarely aimed at her. With her ear pressed against the door, she heard Mrs. Leonard say, "I love you, Mary Ann, and I wish you were my little girl."

It's tempting to want to lend our ears to the voices that speak so loudly in our culture, voices that confuse and clutter our minds, voices that convince us at times that we are of no value to God or his kingdom-building efforts, when really, we are loved and called to live as his children and that knowledge should change everything.

Overview of the Text

In the previous lesson we suggested that the Sermon on the Mount is the Magna Carta for the Kingdom of Christ. Specifically, we looked at two primary rules of God's kingdom on earth: Reversal through the beatitudes and an internal righteousness through Jesus' reinterpretation of the Mosaic code. In this lesson we will look at three more rules from this sermon that are core to the kingdom.

Pondering the Preaching of Jesus

- What kinds of things give you security in life?
- Give the names of three people whose opinions about you really matter to you.
- What was the last thing you did in church for which you were praised?

Meaning of the Text Rule #3: *Praise from God alone (6:1-18)*. Chapter 6 opens with a striking contrast to chapter 5. We were just told to be salt and light (Matt. 5:13-16). Now we're warned not to let people see our good deeds. This may appear contradictory, but it is really speaking of two very different contexts. Chapter 5 deals with social morality; chapter 6 deals with religious activity. Jesus could have given a number of other illustrations but he chose these three particularly Jewish expressions: alms, prayer, and fasting. When we practice such religious duties, Jesus says, we are to do so in such a private way that no one but God would know. If God alone sees, then God alone will be impressed. And if God alone is impressed, then God alone can reward.

It is interesting that our natural tendency is to hide our salt and light but flaunt our religious activities among our fellows. We want the church folk to know just how Christian we are, yet our non-Christian friends often never see our piety. According to rule #3, this is the opposite of what God demands in the kingdom.

The problem with seeking the praise of men through alms, prayer, and fasting (or a host of other religious activities) is that human recognition is fleeting and fickle. Furthermore, if that's what we get, that's all we get. We can choose to seek God's approval or man's but not both.

Now this certainly doesn't mean that there is never a time for corporate prayer. They did that in the book of Acts. Nor does it mean we should not fast as a group or ever know about another's financial gift. Obviously there are examples in the NT of each of these corporate religious activities. All Jesus is saying is that our motives should be to please God, not to receive praise from people. In essence he is doing the same thing here with religious piety that he did in chapter 5 with the Mosaic legal code. He takes the external behavior and demands that it be done with right internal motives.

Doing the right thing is not enough for Jesus. He expects us to do it for the right reason.

Rule #4: *Seeking first (and only) the kingdom (6:19-34)*. Not only are we to look to God alone for approval for piety, we are to look to him alone for daily sustenance. This is a difficult teaching so let's not make it harder than it is. Jesus is not calling us to be poor but to be focused. Certainly Jesus requires us to give to the poor (6:19-21, cf. Luke 12:33). But there is nothing in the text demanding us to be ascetics. Jesus does call for us to be focused. Specifically, we are to serve God, not money. That means we use money to serve God not ourselves (6:24). In order to have that kind of focus we must have a good eye (6:22-23). Literally, we are to have a "single eye"—a single-minded focus on the things of God rather than the things of this world. In short, we are to seek first the kingdom, not the trinkets stocked at Wal-Mart.

In America, dripping with materialistic distractions, this is an incredibly difficult challenge. We are bombarded with materialistic distractions through the cultural norm of the rampant accumulation of wealth. We are expected to own cars, cell phones, shoes, and laptops. We are expected to pay $7 for a movie and wear name brand clothes, to play CDs and invest in the stock market. It's not that any of these are evil, they are merely distracting, and that's where the challenge lies. If it were a choice between good and evil we would see clearly. But choices between good and best confuse us. Jesus demands not merely to be our #1 priority, but our exclusive priority. How difficult this is in our nation where financial harlots seduce us away from our single devotion to God.

Our fear is that, if we don't look out for ourselves, nobody else will. Jesus dispels that myth with two earthly illustrations: Birds and flowers. Doesn't God take care of them? On a scale of 1 to 10 they would probably be near the lower half of the scale. But human beings, particularly king-

18 dom people, are an 11! If wildflowers and sparrows are cared for so well, don't you think God will care for you? Not even Solomon matched the splendor of a simple hillside in spring. And speaking of Solomon, how well did he do spiritually with all his earthly wealth? It seems that the lily is a better example of faith than the wise king.

"Therefore I tell you, do not worry about your life, what you will eat or drink; or about your body, what you will wear. Is not life more important than food, and the body more important than clothes?" (6:25). Worry is practical atheism. It betrays our unbelief in a loving God. We must not call Jesus a liar in this regard. How we handle our finances and our concern over them is one of the best barometers of our trust in Jesus.

Rule #5: *Concluding corollaries: Judging, prayer, and the hard road.* Let's summarize where we've been so far. We are to look to God alone for approval with our piety and for security in our worldly needs. If we do that then several other things will fall into place. If we trust God alone for recognition and security, that frees us in three things. First, we no longer need to judge other people (7:1-6). Now let's get one thing clear about judging. Jesus is not saying that we should never exercise moral discernment. Look again at verse 6. How can you know who's a dog and a pig without making some kind of evaluation? Moreover, Jesus is not interdicting arbitration between brothers. In Matthew 18:15-20, he gives us a model for confronting an erring brother. What Jesus is forbidding here is the kind of judgmentalism that is often common place in religious circles. We make assessments about another's relationship to God based on clothes, language, past, etc. Most of us could never live up to our own standards that we use to measure others. Jesus is saying, "Stop it!" If God is your sole source of self-esteem and security, then you relinquish the need to slam others, to gossip about them, to try to

The Preaching of Jesus

"fix them up." In the kingdom we are freed from criticism, assumptions, and slander. They are simply irrelevant to those who are secure in Christ. *When you stop looking after your own interest, it is amazing how you can keep your nose out of other people's business.*

Second, when we trust God alone for security and reward, we pray much differently. It is amazing, really, how much emphasis there is in this sermon on prayer. We have two major sections that deal with it (6:5-14; 7:7-11). In both of these texts, the key word is "Father." This is truly astounding. Jesus was teaching his disciples to address Yahweh as their personal father. True enough, the Jews did talk about God as the father of the nation. But there is no precedent for addressing him as a personal "Dad." Jesus' teaching on prayer is revolutionary. Not only was it shocking to the Jews, it is unbelievable to most Christians. Oh, I'm not suggesting that Christians don't *use* the word "father" in their prayers . . . we *do*. What I'm suggesting is that we don't *pray* as if God were our father. Having children myself, I know how they ask (with honesty, simplicity, *and persistence*). And I know what they ask for (wants, needs, and dreams). Most of us simply don't pray like that. Why? Because we've not yet caught Jesus' teaching. Because we've not yet made Yahweh our sole source of self-esteem and security.

Finally, if God alone were our source, we would be more willing to take the narrow road (13-27). The broad way is attractive; after all, there are lots of room and lots of people to keep you company (13-14). False prophets take that road. They perform miracles and cast out demons, but they don't know Jesus (15-23). Foolish people build on sand because it is quicker than getting down to the bedrock (24-27). But none of these will survive the storm of God's judgment. The kingdom is open to all, but it is not wide open. It has a narrow road for the single-minded. Its entrance is difficult, and God is its only judge. Until he is our sole source of self-esteem and

The Magna Carta of the Kingdom—Part 2

security, we're not yet fit for the kingdom. Press your ear to this text and I think that is what you will hear.

Practicing the Preaching of Jesus

1. Make a list of the 10 most important things in your life. Pretend you can only keep half; cross the others off the list. Now, you can only keep three; cross two off. You can only keep one; cross two more off. What's left?

2. Revisit your list in the first exercise. Next to each item, write the number of hours you spent obtaining, caring for, or experiencing each item this last week. Are you spending the most time with the things that really matter?

3

> Have courage for the greatest sorrow of life and patience for the small one; and when you have laboriously accomplished your daily task, go to sleep in peace. God is awake.
>
> —*Victor Hugo*

> The kingdom of God is not realm but reign; not domain but dominion.
>
> —*William Newton Clarke*

STORIES OF THE KINGDOM

Text: Matthew 13:1-52 **Memory**: Matthew 13:16-17

Spiritual Nourishment

The *British Weekly* published this letter:

Dear Sir:

It seems ministers feel their sermons are very important and spend a great deal of time preparing them. I have been attending church quite regularly for thirty years, and I have probably heard 3,000 of them. To my consternation, I discovered I cannot remember a single sermon. I wonder if a minister's time might be more profitably spent on something else?

For weeks a storm of editorial responses ensued . . . finally ended by this letter:

Dear Sir:

I have been married for thirty years. During that time I

have eaten 32,850 meals—mostly my wife's cooking. Suddenly I have discovered I cannot remember the menu of a single meal. And yet . . . I have the distinct impression that without them, I would have starved to death long ago.

We would be wise to recognize the spiritual nourishment or value of a lesson or sermon. Especially the ones served up by Jesus.

Overview of the Text

This sermon is composed of eight separate parables. This doesn't mean that what Jesus says is unimportant or fictional. It does, however, make it pretty odd for a sermon. We tend to think of parables as quaint stories for children that are rather simple to grasp. Not so! Jesus' stories are confusing, subversive, and explosive. To string a series of them together is going to make for an extraordinary lesson.

What makes this even more interesting is that each parable is about the kingdom. Just as the kingdom was the core of the Sermon on the Mount, so now it is the topic of each individual parable. There is a difference, however. The Sermon on the Mount gives rules to its citizens about living in the kingdom. These stories trace its contours. Put another way, the Sermon on the Mount is the Magna Carta of the Kingdom, the Sermon in Parables establishes the kingdom's borders.

Pondering the Preaching of Jesus

❉ Give a definition of the word "kingdom."
❉ Historically speaking, what leads to the rise and downfall of most earthly kingdoms?
❉ How would your behavior change if you lived as a citizen of a kingdom rather than a member of a church?

Meaning of the Text Definition of the Kingdom of Heaven:
Whatever else the kingdom of God is, it has something to do with God's real rule. To call it the *kingdom of heaven* neither pushes it to the future nor raises it above the earth. Let me explain. While the kingdom will only be fully manifest after Jesus returns, it has been fully functional since the day of Pentecost. We are in the kingdom NOW . . . yes, even on this earth. To call it a heavenly kingdom describes where God is, not where his rule will be carried out. In fact, the purpose of this kingdom is to announce the introduction of God's rule into Jesus' very real world. He is claiming to be the arbiter and announcer of God's reign in their midst.

Among other things, this means that the church is part of God's administration. Obviously I'm not talking about all those organizational groups that sign leases for buildings and write by-laws for a 501C-3 (tax-exempt status). I'm talking about that preeminent collection of individuals who have entrusted their lives to Jesus and live according to his rule through the power of the Holy Spirit. We're not merely members of a church; we are citizens of a kingdom. We don't own property; we have dominion. We don't follow preachers; we bow before a king. We don't have rules or board meetings, we have laws to live by. Jesus established a heavenly kingdom right here on earth that eagerly anticipates the ultimate manifestation of its sovereign, not in heaven, but on the new earth in the new Jerusalem. But there I go again, getting ahead of myself. Come back to earth and let's take a peak at this heavenly kingdom.

Outline of the Sermon in Parables: What we have here is a collection of eight parables in chiasmic order. What that means is that the first and the last parables go together, the second and seventh go together, likewise the third/fourth and fifth/sixth. Take a look at the chart below. Take time now to read each of the paired parables together out loud. After you read each one, as a group come up with a single sentence that captures the main point of each parable.

> **Chiasmic Outline of the Sermon in Parables**
>
> A Parable of the soils (1-9), purpose of parables (10-17), explanation (18-23)
>   B Parable of the tares and judgment (24-30)
>   C Parables of mustard seed and leaven (31-33)
>   D Private explanation of the tares (36-43)
>   C′ Parables of a treasure in a field and the pearl of great price (44-46)
>   B′ Parable of the dragnet and judgment (47-50)
> A′ Parable of the householder with new and old treasures in the storehouse (51-52)

Notice that two of the parables are explained for you (A. "The Soils," vv. 18-23, and B. "The Tares," vv. 31-33). This should give you insight into how the other parables should be understood. One last observation: The first four parables were spoken in public. The last four were spoken in private after Jesus took his disciples back inside the house. This gives us the impression that his parables, while spoken to the crowd were more pointedly directed to the disciples. This too is instructive. The teaching on the kingdom is deliberately hidden from outsiders. This is deep stuff for those mature enough to handle it. These may be stories, but they are NOT for children or novices.

Lessons from the Sermon in Parables: Volumes of articles and books have been written about Jesus' parables. This is appropriate, since the current of his words runs deep. Here, however, we're simply trying to map out the borders of the kingdom. So we will ask, "What are the major lessons we must learn from this chiasmic collection of stories?"

Lesson #1: From the story of the soils we learn that the message (the seed) is spread broadly but not all will receive it the same. Some receive and believe, others reject it outright,

still others attempt to grow the seed but because of "pollu-
tants" added to the soil the seed is choked out. Mere scatter-
ing doesn't assure productive results. Preaching is essential,
but not sufficient. The soil must be right or the seed will never
mature.

Lesson #2: From the parable of the tares and the drag-
net we learn that judgment (alone) will separate true kingdom
people from people of the world. The kingdom of heaven is
thoroughly entrenched on earth. Yet we are qualitatively different. Kingdom people are saved, while others are damned.
While this vast difference may not be readily apparent here
and now, a day is coming when the discerning angels will
easily sweep the earth and divide God's servants from the
Devil's envoys.

Lesson #3: From the parables of the mustard seed and
leaven we learn that the kingdom may begin as a very small
thing, but it will inevitably grow into something very large.
Jesus surely looked insignificant on the shore of Galilee that
day, yet his prediction continues to unfold as the kingdom of
heaven permeates the earth. There is a relentless increase of
Christianity across the globe that will ultimately usher in the
return of Christ.

Lesson #4: From the parables of the treasure and pearl
we learn that the kingdom is worth giving everything else for.
It's a good thing too since that is precisely what Jesus
requires. There is no dual citizenship in Christ's kingdom. He
demands outrageous and absolute loyalty. But when we have
sacrificed all to gain him, he is a treasure of inestimable
value. We find that when Jesus is all we have, we need nothing else. His person and presence, his rule in our lives, is the
fortune we've been searching for all our lives.

In summary, we preach a kingdom that many reject outright or fail to fulfill. We mustn't let this discourage us. We
live in a world filled with tares and flaky fish. Don't let that
make you let go of the kingdom. Ultimately God will weed the

Stories of the Kingdom

wicked from our midst and establish his eschatological kingdom. For now it is enough to know that in an imperfect and often hostile world, the kingdom continues to grow and our treasure is more than enough to sustain us.

Practicing the Preaching of Jesus

As a group or on your own, take each of these parables and retool them using language relevant to an audience in our culture. Be able to explain them in a way that today's listener would recognize their value and intent.

4

4   **4**

> The true character of a man is seen in what he does for those who can do nothing for him.
>
> —Anonymous

THE GREATEST IN THE KINGDOM

4   **4**

Text: Matthew 20:20-28; Mark 9:33-37; Luke 22:24-27

Memory: Matthew 20:26-28

The Appearance of Greatness

A newly promoted colonel had moved into a makeshift office during the Gulf War. He was just getting unpacked when out of the corner of his eye, he noticed a private coming his way with a toolbox.

Wanting to seem important, he grabbed the phone. "Yes, General Schwarzkopf, I think that's an excellent plan." He continued, "You've got my support on it. Thanks for checking with me. Let's touch base again soon, Norm. Goodbye."

"And what can I do for you?" he asked the private.

"Ahhh, I'm just here to hook up your phone," came the rather sheepish reply.

28 **Overview of the Text**

Chickens aren't the only animals with a pecking order. Dogs, water buffalo, hyenas, goats, and lions all share this affinity for priority. In humans, this is one of our baser instincts. It goes well beyond a need for social order or personal recognition. We desire to dominate, not just lead. We crave for our fellows to cower in deference to our superiority. Yet this desire is antithetical to the cross of Christ. His power was in suffering, his leadership in service. What's more, his admonitions to us on greatness always follow on the heels of his predictions about his own passion. Thus, the cross is not merely an historical event for Jesus, it is a way of life and leadership that he ordained for us to follow.

Pondering the Preaching of Jesus

✴ When a person chooses to be selfless, are they always taken advantage of?

✴ In what ways is it important for you to be recognized? Is there anyone whose attention you most seek?

✴ Is there anyone you are competing with in life? If so, why?

Meaning of the Text

On three separate occasions the Gospels record this argument among the Apostles: which was the greatest? One can only imagine how it got started. Nathanael might have recalled (with a smirk of superiority, of course) how Jesus called him an Israelite without guile. Philip would clear his throat knowingly and remind him who met Jesus first and the fact that Nathanael never would have met Jesus if it weren't for his leadership. Matthew would say something about being more seeker-sensitive than the rest, which would set Simon the Zealot into a frenzied discourse on truth, courage, and sacrifice. Peter pipes in about some water-walking record. James and John remind their former business partner, that they have the majority vote in the inner three. Their mother, Salome, nods vigorously over their shoulders in recognition. Andrew sits quietly seething. Of course Judas Iscariot puts his two cents in . . . something about Jesus trusting him with the finances.

For our part, we stand aghast. We just can't imagine that spiritual men would act like children vying to ride shotgun to the mall. How can Jesus' handpicked leaders be so crassly arrogant and self-seeking? To answer that question, we must make several observations.

First, this idea of humble service is a new teaching. Jesus is introducing a way of leadership that is all too familiar to modern Christians but was a radically new concept to the twelve. They never had a model of one leading through service. They didn't live in a culture of humility.

Second, the system of shame/honor was embedded into their social fabric. Pecking order was essential in every village and family. It was part of marketplace greetings, synagogue assignments, and seating charts at banquets. Moreover, there was little opportunity for upward mobility. Everyone in your social circle knew where s/he belonged and stayed there pretty much all his or her life. To complicate matters, there was an underlying assumption that "honor" was a limited resource. That is, there's only so much to be spread around. And if someone raised in status, then s/he had to get it from somewhere. In other words, if someone goes up, another must go down. Suddenly the Apostles find themselves in a new social group where the pecking order has not yet been established. According to every impulse of their upbringing, this is something worth fighting for.

Third, while we conceal our motives better than the Apostles, we are hardly less vigilant in looking out for our own aggrandizement. Perhaps we are subtler, but certainly no less concerned with self-promotion. From business cards to

The Greatest in the Kingdom

30 parking places, from titles to degrees, we make sure our names are known and our accomplishments recognized. We come by it naturally, of course. From our earliest childhood we have been through the boot camp of self-assertion. Grandparents spoiled us, soccer moms screamed like warring Scythians every time we touched the ball. Teachers gave us gold stars, and coaches showered us with trophies, all the while screaming, "Get aggressive out there!" It's no wonder we spend so much time thinking, plotting, and dreaming about our next foray into the limelight.

I suppose that's why Jesus' teaching on humility is so difficult—it goes against our basic training. Perhaps that's why it's repeated three times; God knew we needed to be pummeled with it. Take a look at our texts. On three separate occasions we read about this argument. You know what is really shocking? Go back and read what Jesus says just prior to the Apostles' argument (Matt. 20:17-19; Mark 9:31-32; Luke 22:19-23). Each time Jesus has just predicted his own death. He promises to lay down his life for these men and they're arguing about which is the greatest. Look also at what follows each argument (Matt. 20:25-28; Mark 9:35-37; Luke 22:25-27). It is a pretty stern rebuke. There is a consistent pattern here. Jesus predicts his death, the disciples argue about who is the greatest, and Jesus rebukes them for misunderstanding his whole mission.

This pattern is embarrassing enough, but it climaxes during the last supper. Jesus has washed the disciples' feet in an outrageous act of service. He has distributed the emblems of the Passover meal and transformed them into a Communion celebration. He has clarified his death and established a new covenant. But what do they do? The wine of the Eucharist is still dripping from their lips as they argue over their own greatness. Outrageous! Jesus' heart must have been broken. In fact, one wonders if this isn't why he predicted at that very moment his betrayal by Peter (Luke 22:31-

34). One wonders, too, if our own attempts at self-promotion are any less offensive in the shadow of the cross, if they are any less ill-conceived or ill-timed.

Jesus' death for us was not merely an event for us to appreciate and appropriate. It was a pattern he established and expects us to follow. After all, we are to take up our crosses and follow Jesus (Matt. 10:38). We are to be crucified with Christ (Gal. 2:20). Why do we imagine that we can be crucified with certain honors that were stripped from Jesus? Why do we attempt to wear merit badges to our execution? How can we possibly claim to follow Jesus if we pretend we are in an honor parade rather than a death march? Our lives are ludicrous when we grapple for recognition and position, all the while imagining that we are grasping Jesus' intention for our lives.

During World War II, England needed to increase its production of coal. Winston Churchill called together labor leaders to enlist their support. At the end of his presentation he asked them to picture in their minds a parade which would be held after the war was won. First, he said, would come the sailors who had kept the vital sea lanes open. Then would come the soldiers who had come home from Dunkirk and then gone on to defeat Rommel in Africa. Then would come the pilots who had driven the Luftwaffe from the sky.

Last of all, he said, would come a long line of sweat-stained, soot-streaked men in miner's caps. Someone would cry from the crowd, "And where were you during the critical days of our struggle?"

And ten thousand voices would shout the answer, "We were deep in the earth with our faces to the coal."

Let's clarify one last point. Jesus does call us to be leaders. He does offer us greatness, success, reward, and power. Our goal is no different than the world's—we want to be great, we want to win. . . . God wants that for us as well. It is not our goal that is different but our method of achieving that

The Greatest in the Kingdom

32 goal. The world teaches its children to fight for it through self-promotion, shrewd posturing, and vicious backbiting. And frankly, these methods make a lot of sense. Plot it on graph paper and you can see how this would accomplish your goals. However, Jesus offered a different means to greatness. Lay down your life, serve others, get dirty in the coal mines so to speak, but let God alone recognize and reward you. It is so ridiculous, so outrageous, so countercultural and paradoxical, it just might work.

Practicing the Preaching of Jesus

Develop a plan for your church body that will demonstrate this line of thinking to an unbelieving community. Look at your calendar and strategically organize events that will serve to better the community you live in. Paint someone's house, adopt a segment of the highway to clean up, have a free car wash, feed people once a week in the church basement, sponsor a 3-on-3 basketball tournament or a 5K race. Be proactive in serving others and do it in a way that doesn't just target one segment of your community's population, but all of them in a way that is disarming. Your church will grow numerically and spiritually!

THE GOOD SAMARITAN —A NEW DEFINITION OF HUMANITY

> What value has compassion that does not take its object in its arms?
>
> —Antoine de Saint-Exupery

> It is one of the beautiful compensations of this life that no one can sincerely try to help another without helping himself.
>
> —Charles Dudley Warner

> Goodness is uneventful. It does not flash, it glows.
>
> —David Grayson

Text: Luke 10:25-37   **Memory:** Luke 10:36-37

The Testimony of Compassion

While serving with Operation Mobilization in India in 1967, Doug Nichols was forced into a sanitarium for several months because of a complicated case of tuberculosis. Many of the other patients in the ward were not thrilled with the idea of a rich, young American taking up bed space in a free, government-run sanitarium. Nichols didn't speak the language but did his best to reach out to the other patients by trying to give them literature in their language. Everyone he encountered politely refused.

The first few nights were restless. He woke up around 2:00 A.M. coughing. One morning during a coughing spell, he noticed one of the older and sicker patients across the aisle trying to get out of bed. He would sit up on the edge of the bed and try to stand, but in weakness would fall back into bed

34 and cry softly. Doug Nichols wasn't sure what the man was trying to accomplish.

The next morning Nichols realized the older patient had been trying to get up and walk to the bathroom. The stench in their ward was awful. Other patients yelled insults at the man. Angry nurses moved him roughly from side to side as they cleaned up the mess. One nurse even went so far as to slap him. The old man curled up into a ball, defeated, and wept.

The next night the young American woke up with another spell of coughing brought on by his tuberculosis. He again saw the older man trying to get out of his bed. Like the previous night, he fell back whimpering. Nichols, though himself weakened, got out of bed and went over to him. He smiled, put his arms under the older man and picked him up. He carried the man to the washroom, which was a filthy, small room with a hole in the floor. He stood behind the frail and feeble man as the man took care of himself. After he finished, Nichols picked him up again and carried him back to his bed. As he laid him down, the elderly man kissed him on the cheek, smiled, and said something Nichols couldn't understand.

The next morning, Nichols felt a tug on his shirt. When he opened his eyes, he was surprised to see a group of patients gathered around his bed. They were all smiling as one of their number handed him a cup of hot tea. The group of patients then made it known that they were eager to read the tracts Nichols had attempted to give them earlier in the week.

It wasn't good health or persuasive speech or a strategic plan that reached those patients. Rather, it was a man who was willing to do something no one else would do, and that was simply to make a trip to the bathroom.

Overview of the Text

This legal expert could hardly have asked Jesus a more important question: "What must I do to be saved?" Yet he could hardly have asked it with more insidious motives—to test Jesus (v. 25). He was one in a long line of pharisaic challengers who

The Preaching of Jesus

tried to trap Jesus. With a lesser question we might have the leisure to be impressed with Jesus' intellectual prowess or oratory skill. With such an important question on the table, however, and with such a momentous response, all we can do is marvel and tremble at Jesus' new definition of humanity and our obligation to it.

Pondering the Preaching of Jesus

- In your community, whom do you often overlook?
- Have you ever caught yourself saying, "They deserve what they've gotten" or "They're not my responsibility" toward a certain segment of the population?
- Who is your neighbor? Name specific people.

Meaning of the Text

He is called a lawyer. However, he's not wearing the pinstriped suit of Washington, but a prayer shawl and phylacteries. He's an expert in the Mosaic law. Indeed, he *is* involved in litigation and debates but they are thoroughly enmeshed in the religious world of Judaism, not merely the civil law of society at large. In this context he accosts Jesus with an important question, indeed, *the* most important question: "What must I do to inherit eternal life?"

This was obviously not an uncommon question. Rabbis and theologians had been bantering it back and forth for eons. Even today religious leaders argue vociferously over the entrance requirements for heaven. Rather than entering the debate cold turkey, Jesus asks the lawyer to direct the discussion with his own answer to the question. The young lawyer's answer was excellent. In fact, he identified the very mandates that Jesus himself would later call the greatest two commandments (Matt. 22:37-40). To love God and to love our neighbors encompasses the heart of all the laws of the Old Testament (Matt. 7:12; 22:36-40; Rom. 13:8-10; Gal. 5:14; Jas. 2:8). He nailed it . . . but now it's his turn to be nailed.

Jesus replies, "Do this and you will live." Suddenly, rather than Jesus being under fire, the lawyer is under the gun. Feeling the pressure he wants to lighten the load. So to justify himself he asks a second question: "Who is my neighbor?" Now that's an interesting question. You see, the word "neighbor" literally means "one near." The intent of this man's question, therefore, is to restrict the command by limiting those who would qualify as a "near" person. Is a fellow Israelite who lives in Jericho my neighbor or is he too far away? Or perhaps I should limit the neighborhood to just my town or barrio. Maybe my neighbor is only a person who lives on my street. Going a different direction, we might constrict "my neighbor" to a person who dresses like me, has my political or religious affiliations, or who shares my interests, social status, or economic standing. "You see," the lawyer would say, "we must know what the definition of 'is' is." His question, in classic lawyerese, is quite slippery. Jesus' response is about to undo him.

Rather than stepping into a slippery question, Jesus hovers above it with a story. It is quite a tale too. It has twists and turns, intrigue, danger, and a surprise ending. You know the basic plot. A man travels the treacherous highway from Jerusalem to Jericho. It was a desert road that descended nearly 3,000 feet. It is peppered with caves and riddled with bandits, as our main character will soon find out. He is beaten, robbed, and left for dead. Our naked and bloodied protagonist needs 911. He'll not have to wait long. Following a short distance behind him was a priest. He had apparently just completed his biannual week of service in the Holy City. Bathed in prayer and filled with images of God's worshiping people, he returns home to carry out his normal routine. His quiet trek is interrupted. He is faced with a huddled mass. His mind begins to race, "He's been robbed! I wonder where they are? I wonder if he's dead?" Faced with the dilemma of benevolence or common sense, he chooses the latter and scurries on by.

The Preaching of Jesus

A second "holy man" comes along. This one is a Levite—same class of clergy, but more specifically tied to the Aaronic priesthood. Yet he's no more committed to alleviating human suffering than his colleague.

A third traveler passes by; this one was a Samaritan. Now, I realize that we call this story "The Parable of the Good Samaritan." The fact is, however, that in the eyes of this lawyer there was no such thing. Samaritans were the neighbors to the north, a despised group of "half-breeds" that frequently bore the brunt of Jewish racism and returned it in kind. This history of animosity is not worth repeating here, but suffice to say it was long and deeply entrenched. In a shocking (even offensive) twist, Jesus has the Samaritan care for this man's needs *out of his own resources!* It is simply outrageous.

Jesus' conclusion radically realigns the lawyer's question in two significant ways. First, the lawyer asked, "Who is near enough to me that I would be obligated to love him?" In other words, he wants to draw the circle in as tight as it could possibly go so he can minimize his obligation and yet still be saved. Oddly, Jesus allows the circle to be drawn into an 18-inch diameter. He says, "Your neighbor is that person immediately next to you." However, the circle has to go with you! Instead of using a mirror to determine your neighbor by those that look like you, you use a periscope to locate those individuals you might run into.

The second radical realignment of the question is that Jesus turns "neighbor" from a noun to a verb. Being a neighbor is not something you are, it is something you do. Listen again to Jesus' conclusion (v. 36): "Which of these three do you think *was a neighbor* to the man who fell into the hands of robbers?" Being a neighbor is not an issue of identification but action. The lawyer was asking about being near another person, Jesus answered about being there for another person.

This is perhaps the most important story Jesus ever told. Not only does it deal with the issue of who is saved, but it

The Good Samaritan—A New Definition of Humanity

practically and poignantly delineates our obligation to others. Humanity is no longer defined by proximity but need. If we are to be godly, we must be thoroughly enmeshed in humanity. Dangerously, blindly, and sacrificially, we must engage a world that is beaten, bloodied, and naked. And if we don't, we must question the status of our salvation. This is not to say that heaven is contingent on our benevolence. It is rather to suggest that practical, even radical compassion is an inevitable result of a right relationship with God. In fact, this parable doesn't merely answer, "How do I love my neighbor?" but also, "How can I appropriately express my love for God?" How can one claim to love God whom they have not seen without loving their neighbor whom they have seen? (1 John 4:20).

Practicing the Preaching of Jesus

Evaluate the physical needs of the community you live in. Make a list of those needs that could be met by your church. Rank the needs according to which ones need to be addressed immediately and which ones don't require immediate attention. Pray for a plan, educate your church family, build your teams, and implement the plan by a target date. The chart below could be used as a model for how your exercise could be fulfilled.

Rank	Need	Helpers	Action Plan (yes/no)	Date

THE GOOD SHEPHERD— JESUS' VICIOUS COMPASSION

> God tempers the wind to the shorn lamb.
> —Henri Estienne
>
> There is no exercise better for the heart than reaching down and lifting people up.
> —John Andrew Holmer
>
> Biblical orthodoxy without compassion is surely the ugliest thing in the world.
> —Francis A. Schaeffer

Text: John 10:1-21　　　　　　**Memory:** John 10:11,18

Eccentric Compassion When narcotics squad detectives recently raided a loft apartment in a depressed area of New York City, they came on a scene straight out of "The Beggar's Opera." Every square foot of the long, dingy apartment was crowded with human derelicts who were sleeping on the floor or sitting huddled in corners; dimly visible overhead were a number of paper ceiling ornaments, left over from the days when the loft had been a dance hall. After searching the crowd, the detectives arrested six men who were carrying hypodermic needles and packets of heroin; they also arrested the addict's host, a mild-mannered man who was charged with harboring drug addicts in his apartment.

At police headquarters, the owner of the loft apartment claimed he was actually a well-to-do heir, but that he had chosen to live among the homeless in order to provide them with food, shelter, and clothing. His door, he said, was open to all, including a small minority of narcotics addicts. He didn't know that it was against the law to feed and clothe people with drug habits. Checking his story, the police found that the man was indeed neither a vagrant nor a drug addict. He was John Sargent Cram, a millionaire who had been educated at Princeton and Oxford and whose family had long been noted for its philanthropies. Wishing to avoid the rigmarole of organized charity work, Cram had simply moved into the loft and set about helping the homeless directly, at a cost of $100 or so a day. He made a point of not giving the men money, instead he invested emotional stock in the men, loving them and showing them their potential. He later told reporters, "I don't know that my work does much good, but I don't think it does any harm. I'm quite happy. I'm anything but a despondent person. Call me eccentric. Call it my reason for being. I have no other."

Jesus made the choice to invest in our futures, to come alongside a dirty, homeless humanity. His compassion for directionless people like you and me wasn't always accepted by those who policed Judaism. In their eyes, Jesus' words and associations with the down and out seemed eccentric. But from God's vantage point, they seemed to be his reason for being.

Overview of the Text

Never were more comforting words spoken, "I am the good shepherd." They should be accompanied with a quiet string quartet or the gentle lullaby of a nursery. They're not! They are surrounded by timpani drums and clashing cymbals. The setting for this scene is not a serene countryside with Jesus encircled by his closest followers. No, this is smack-dab in the middle of the temple with the aggressive din of Jesus' enemies encircling him. This is a hostile scene with a violent response. While these words *do* comfort the disciples, they were originally a threat, not a promise. As the Pharisees attempt to

Pondering the Preaching of Jesus

- ✴ Share a time that someone fought for you. How did that make you feel?
- ✴ Take the time to read through John 7–9 out loud. Have one person write down each text that describes the tension between Jesus and the Jewish leaders. Have another person write down all the claims Jesus makes.
- ✴ Read through this sermon (John 10:1-21). Find all the advantages you can to being in Jesus' flock. Brainstorm about other passages that also promise the same kind of provision to Christians.

Meaning of the Text

Six months prior to the final Passover Jesus returns to Jerusalem after a hiatus of eighteen months. The city is buzzing. Everyone wants to know if the controversial Galilean will make another appearance. In fact, even his brothers prodded him to go (John 7:1-11). After all, a would-be Messiah should stake his claim in the capital city, not in the back woods of Galilee. To the delight of many, as well as the consternation of not a few, Jesus shows up halfway through the Feast of Tabernacles. The fireworks begin immediately.

For several days Jesus and the leaders go head to head. In every foray the leaders are bested by this peasant from Galilee. What makes it worse is they have home-field advantage, and he is still beating them at their own game. They are baffled by his wisdom (John 7:15) and paralyzed by his words (7:46). Although they persistently tried to kill him, they seemed to be hog-tied by the sovereign hand of God (John 5:18; 7:1,19-20,25,30,32,44-45; 8:59; 9:22; 10:31,39). These heavyweights keep coming at each other no less relentlessly than the Hatfields and McCoys. Their debate culminates in this last address just before Jesus flees. He has been using the rhetoric of debate. For the final foray, however, he shifts into allegory. The innocence of this simple metaphor mustn't conceal Jesus' vicious compassion for his faithful followers.

Jesus uses the familiar image of the shepherd. Now in real life these guys were poor and dirty—defiled by their daily duties. In the symbolic world of biblical imagery, however, shepherds could hardly be held in higher esteem. It's a role occupied by God (Ps 23; 79:13; 95:7), his delegated leaders (Ezek 34:1-6), and his envoy—the Messiah (Ezek 34:23). This, of course, makes Jesus' claim both spectacular and highly controversial. It also makes his claim vivid and unmistakably clear. Everyone in Palestine knew how all this worked.

Sheep were kept in pens at night, which were really nothing more than low stone walls with a small opening on one side. Each evening the flock was ushered into the enclosure. Either the shepherd himself, or a hired watchman, would lay down in front of the door. That way no sheep could get out, nor could predators get in, except, of course, by crossing the shepherd. Thus, if a thief or wolf wanted to attack the sheep, they had to climb the wall (at considerable personal risk, of course).

Each morning the shepherd would call the sheep to follow him to pasture. This is interesting because in most places around the world, sheep are driven. But in the Middle East, they are led. Now the only way to do that is to train the sheep to respond to your voice. You do that by naming each lamb and caring for it tenderly. It learns to follow the voice of the shepherd for provision and protection. Even when several flocks are boarded in the same pen, each sheep will only follow its own shepherd's voice. It is really quite extraordinary.

Against this cultural background, Jesus makes some striking claims. He says, "I am the good (*kalos*) shepherd." Literally, he is the "beautiful" or "fitting" shepherd. He is beautiful because he protects his sheep from predators and thieves.

Moreover he distinguishes himself from all other "supposed" shepherds. The "hirelings" were false shepherds because they only wanted to take from the flock what would benefit themselves whether it was wool or meat. Even worse, when danger reared its ugly head, they fled. Jesus, in contrast, lays down his life to offer salvation to the flock of God. So, Jesus is claiming to offer salvation to the flock of God and he is claiming that others who call themselves shepherds are really the enemy.

Who is this enemy? Well, according to the allegory, these false shepherds, wolves, and thieves are identified as Satan and his underlings, *the Pharisees*! (9:40). As you can imagine, that didn't go over so well. In fact, they replied by calling Jesus demonic (v. 20). It is easy for us to imagine these Pharisees with red eyes and horns. But the truth is they were good religious men. They were the pillars of conservative Judaism, well respected, even revered by the average Joseph. It is no wonder, therefore, that many were confused about which side to take. Many in the crowd loved Jesus, but they also grew up respecting the rabbis who had taught them the Torah. They would be comfortable loving Jesus AND the Pharisees, but Jesus is forcing them into an "either/or" decision. No wonder the crowds were divided (v. 19-21).

It would be unfair to villainize the Pharisees. Yet it would also be unrealistic to pretend that all religious teachers are equally correct. Jesus simply doesn't allow us the luxury of politically correct pluralism. He makes exclusive and outrageous claims. He says that he alone offers salvation to God's flock and all others who counter and compete with him are thieves and liars, detrimental, even deadly, to the sheep. There is one voice we're allowed to listen to. To follow another is to invite disaster.

Jesus' words, on the surface, sound so tender. That's because we listen to them as sheep. But they were spoken among wolves. Originally these were not words to beleaguered believers. These are death threats to enemies. In

The Good Shepherd—Jesus' Vicious Compassion

essence, Jesus is saying, "You think you're gonna steal my sheep?! Over my dead body!" Actually, even his dead body didn't dissuade Jesus' sheep from following him.

For those who listen, for the sheep that follow, there is a decided advantage: Life to the full! (v. 10). This is a life of abundance and protection. It's an extraordinary promise. What makes it even more meaningful is the fact that its genesis is amidst opposition. So too, its fulfillment is not some surreal, pristine life that one only reads about in novels. Rather, in the midst of our very real struggles, amidst controversy and opposition, the Shepherd shows up with glaring eyes and raised staff protecting his people against the enemies of his fold.

Practicing the Preaching of Jesus

Write a poem or prayer to Jesus from the perspective of a wayward sheep just recently rescued from a wolf by the strong hand of the shepherd.

WHEN ANGELS DANCE AND FATHERS RUN

> You can give without loving, but you cannot love without giving.
> —Amy Carmichael

> An atheist does not find God for the same reason a thief does not find a policeman. He is not looking for him.
> —Wendell Baxter

> God creates out of nothing. Therefore until a man is nothing, God can make nothing out of him.
> —Martin Luther

Text: Luke 15:1-32   **Memory**: Luke 15:7

Come Home   Maria's husband had died when Christina was an infant. The young mother, stubbornly refusing opportunities to remarry, got a job and set out to raise her young daughter. And now, fifteen years later, the worst years were over. Though Maria's salary as a maid afforded few luxuries, it was reliable and it did provide food and clothes. And now Christina was old enough to get a job to help out. . . .

She spoke often of going to the city. She dreamed of trading her dusty neighborhood for exciting avenues and city life. Just the thought of this horrified her mother. Maria was always quick to remind Christina of the harshness of the streets. "People don't know you there. Jobs are scarce and the life is cruel. And besides, if you went there, what would you do for a living?"

Maria knew exactly what Christina would do, or would *have* to do for a living. That's why her heart broke when she awoke one morning to find her daughter's bed empty. Maria knew immediately where her daughter had gone. She also knew immediately what she must do to find her. She quickly threw some clothes in a bag, gathered up all her money, and ran out of the house.

On her way to the bus stop she entered a drugstore to get one last things. Pictures. She sat in the photograph booth, closed the curtain, and spent all she could on pictures of herself. With her purse full of small black-and-white photos, she boarded the next bus to Rio de Janeiro.

Maria knew Christina had no way of earning money. She also knew that her daughter was too stubborn to give up. When pride meets hunger, a human will do things that before were unthinkable. Knowing this, Maria began her search. Bars, hotels, nightclubs, any place with the reputation for street walkers or prostitutes. She went to them all. And at each place she left her picture — taped on a bathroom mirror, tacked to a hotel bulletin board, fastened to a corner phone booth. And on the back of each photo she wrote a note. . . .

It was a few weeks later that young Christina descended the hotel stairs. Her young face was tired. Her brown eyes no longer danced with youth but spoke of pain and fear. Her laughter was broken. Her dream had become a nightmare. A thousand times over she had longed to trade these countless beds for her secure pallet. Yet the little village was, in too many ways, too far away.

As she reached the bottom of the stairs, her eyes noticed a familiar face. She looked again, and there on the lobby mirror was a small picture of her mother. Christina's eyes burned and her throat tightened as she walked across the room and removed the small photo. Written on the back was this compelling invitation. "Whatever you have done, whatever you have become, it doesn't matter. Please come home."

She did.[2]

The Preaching of Jesus

Overview of the Text

What can make an angel dance and God run? Nothing but the salvation of one lost soul. Here, in a trilogy of parables, Jesus paints a picture of divine jubilation using a lost sheep, a lost coin, and a lost son. God is unreasonable in his expressions of joy and the angels are downright giddy. Why? Because God loves people. It's that simple, God loves people. He's simply crazy about us.

Pondering the Preaching of Jesus

- Who has been the most forgiving person in your life?
- Whom do you know that has made a decision to follow Christ and you never imagined s/he would?
- Whom do you know that grew up with an understanding of the love of God, but has strayed from God's plan for his/her life? What do you need to do to help him/her get back on track?

Meaning of the Text

He would eat with just about anybody—tax collectors, prostitutes, uneducated peasants. That irked a good number of folks, particularly the religious elite, who were used to having exclusive rights to important people and were put off by being shunned for the likes of these losers. To make matters worse, Jesus was giving these scalawags the false impression that they too could enter the kingdom of God. In fact, not only could they enter, Jesus acted like God would cherish them. This simply wouldn't do, so the religious leaders confronted Jesus about it.

In the fifteenth chapter of Luke we see Jesus surrounded by two groups that mixed about as well as oil and water. On one side were the Pharisees: straight-laced, bedecked with prayer shawls and phylacteries. On the other side were the misfits—drunkards, sleazy women, and other miscellaneous sinners, you know, the kind of folks with tattoos and body piercings. Jesus seemed to get a real kick out of hanging around these sorts. A civil war nearly broke out between the two sides when the upright side got downright uptight over Jesus' open acceptance of the down-and-out.

The Master responds with a trilogy of parables that have become all too familiar. I say deliberately that we have become all too familiar with these stories. As I look around, I still see a homogeneous church filled with folks from the wrong side of the divide. The fact is, we would be no less scandalized today than the Pharisees were by the *hoi polloi* that Jesus welcomed. The institutional church is hardly more welcoming to the dregs of society. The lifeboat has indeed been reconfigured into a yacht.

Yet this theme of love for the least and the lost is key to Jesus' theology. After all, he repeated it three times using imagery familiar to his audience. He gives one story that is particularly male in orientation (lost sheep), one particularly female (lost coin/dowry), and one for the whole family (lost son). Nobody could miss his point! He even punctuated it with dancing angels! You know what is really strange about all this? The more we tell the story, the more we feel justified to ignore its very real implications. It's almost like we've vaccinated ourselves with the very antidote of love.

To see how vitally important this is to the heart of God, we must notice three points in the third parable that are outrageously countercultural. First, no father in the Middle East would actually grant such a foolish request from an idiot son. To give him half the inheritance would require selling off part of the farm which was a birthright. The boy was not entitled to this until after his father's death. Even to ask for it is tantamount to telling the old man to drop dead. Giving in to a rebellious and wayward son is a sure way to lose your assets as well as your cherished respect in the community. The boy would be the grist for gossip, and the father becomes a laughingstock.

Second, Middle Eastern men simply did not run. It was a sign of indignity. The only time to run was when chased by an overpowering enemy or when ordered to do so by your superior. Therefore, anyone who ran was not seen as physically fit but socially degraded. Sissies and slaves ran, not fathers who owned estates. Yet there he is, like Forest Gump, with his long robe girded about his loins, clumping along hurriedly to a grungy son.

Third, a father who had suffered such indignity and shame at the hand of his son, would not welcome him back. And even if he did, there would be a price to pay. Some penalty had to atone for such disobedience. Even if the father didn't want to lash out, he would be obliged by social mores lest he be perceived as spineless and gullible. Yet this father wraps his arms around the boy's putrid shoulders. The stench of swine didn't dissuade his open affection. With a clap of his hand he began to bark out orders to the servant to fetch the boy a pair of sandals, a new robe, and a signet ring as symbols of his status as a son. This wayward child doesn't even have time to finish his well-polished apology. The father is disinterested in all that. His joy overwhelmed him, for the lost son had returned home.

Arguably, this is the greatest short story ever told. It captures our imagination. We can just see the son sulking back home and the father, with reckless abandon, racing to reclaim his prized child. It warms the heart. But there's another shoe left to fall. This story is as much about God the father as it is the sinner-son. The portrait painted of God is not what one would expect. In fact, while this story has been called the "Prodigal Son," it would be more aptly labeled, "The Prodigal Father." After all, it was the father who was more recklessly lavish than the boy. He is the one who took the real risk. He is the one with the costlier love, the one who suffered the most indignity. We can talk about the sovereignty of God and his untouchable transcendence if we want to. But perhaps that's best left to theologians who've never lost a child. Jesus doesn't paint his father in those strokes. Of

When Angels Dance and Fathers Run

course he's still creator, ruler, and sustainer of the universe. Of course he's meticulously executing his cosmic plan. That goes without saying. But God is not a sovereign who is untouched by our affection; he's not unmoved by our rebellion or repentance. Perhaps it's too shocking to even fathom, perhaps so unimaginable that it borders on heresy, but it looks for all the world like *God is vulnerable to our love*. He's not immovable. He runs to us. He ignores propriety and acts in ways that are . . . well, undignified, like putting on skin and hanging on a cross. God's love caused him to be reckless, to grant us our freedom that landed us in a pigsty, with the hope that, against all odds, we would find our way home. For those of us that did, we watch him run, bounding across the landscape, ignoring the vestiges of the sty, and incorporating us back into his household. Oh, God knows the cost. He's going to be shamed for honoring us. The truth is, we will not always represent him well. Yet he doesn't seem to care. Our giddy Father is recklessly in love with us and certainly willing to defend his actions to another son who got lost at home.

Why such risk? Why suffer such indignity at our expense? Put it on a spreadsheet and it hardly adds up. All I can figure is that Yahweh really does love us so much that he just can't help himself. This makes him neither less God nor more human, just more vulnerable, majestic, and fiercer than I formerly imagined.

Practicing the Preaching of Jesus

Watch the movie, "The Mission," (with Robert DeNiro and Jeremy Irons) and discuss it with your group.

8   8

> The reason why Christ chose the hard way of the cross was, among other things, that he saw beyond it.
> —S.J. Reid

> To be crucified means, first, the man on the cross is facing only one direction; second, he is not going back; and third, he has no further plans of his own.
> —A.W. Tozer

THE COST

OF

DISCIPLESHIP

8   8

Text: Luke 14:25-35   **Memory**: Luke 14:26-27

The Need for Challenge

During the height of the Civil War, Abraham Lincoln often found refuge at a Presbyterian Church in Washington, D.C. He would attend with an aide, sit with stovepipe hat in his lap, and do his best not to draw attention to himself. As the preacher delivered his sermon, President Lincoln listened intently, hoping to gain some insight on how to manage his own life and how to govern a nation. The war was tearing the nation and his heart in two. Having recently lost his own son, the president was counting the cost of continuing the war.

One particular Sunday as the pastor finished his sermon, the president and his young assistant quietly exited the little building. The young man asked President Lincoln, "What did you think of today's sermon?" Lincoln responded, "I thought the sermon was carefully thought through and eloquently delivered." The aide quickly shot back, "So you thought it was a great sermon?" The president smiled, stopped walking, and said, "No, I thought the preacher failed." The young assistant was taken back by his harsh critique and said, "How did he fail? Why did he fail?" President Lincoln paused for a moment, then spoke quietly, but firmly, "He failed because he did not ask of us something great."

Overview of the Text

At the apex of Jesus' popularity, he laid down his most radical requirements for discipleship. The crowds were streaming to him. Most teachers would be mesmerized by such affection. Jesus, however, seemed a bit put out. He doesn't appear to be interested in the number of his followers but the depth of their commitment. He doesn't merely ask for ultimate sacrifice, but absolute loyalty. He demands our resignation of family, lands, even life itself.

Pondering the Preaching of Jesus

✴ How have we reduced Jesus' radical demands of discipleship in order to make becoming a Christian easier? What do people in your church think Jesus requires to be a follower?

✴ Why do you think churches soft-pedal Jesus?

✴ Read Luke 14:25-27 along with Matthew 19:29. Make a list of all the things Jesus calls us to leave. Which has been the hardest for you? What are you still holding onto?

Meaning of the Text

Popular singers or preachers are often said to have the crowd in the palm of their hand. The truth, more often than not, is that the crowds have the performer in their pocket. They control how he feels about himself. They dictate her financial stability or her very movements. Popularity has a way of intoxicating its victims. Jesus, however, seems thoroughly disinterested in accolades and untouched by adoration. At this point he's most popular, yet here he becomes the most demanding of his followers.

"If you want to follow me," he says, "I must have your absolute loyalty." He then specifies the loyalty he demands in two specific categories. First, you must hate your father and mother, wife and children, sister and brother. Now, we've all heard that the word "hate" is relative here (pardon the pun). Jesus is not saying to have antipathy toward your family, rather he is saying that compared to our love for him, it will look like, and perhaps feel like hate to them. This is mostly true but needs clarification.

In the social context of first-century Judaism, the family was the core social unit. It was obligatory to support and defend the family. If one didn't, s/he was considered a heretical outcast. The family was the source of financial stability and social networks. In contrast, our families are so scattered that most of us find our primary social circle in our friends and coworkers. It is, therefore, difficult for us to appreciate the unmitigated fidelity of the Jewish family. The "clan" was essential. To step outside it was to be a pariah. Therefore, what Jesus is demanding is that we change allegiances from our biological family to our spiritual-adoptive family. To do so meant that one would turn his back on the core social unit. It is like an athlete who quits the team to play for another or a business partner who sells out to work with the competition.

To abandon family in Jesus' day would be tantamount to joining a cult group today. Thus, Jesus' use of the word "hate" is entirely appropriate and completely literal. Oh, it might not describe how the Christian *feels*, but it certainly describes how their behavior would be *perceived*. By this I do not intend to say that the abandoned family thinks we hate them because we really don't. I'm not talking about feelings but behavior. Our behavior would be justifiably described as

The Cost of Discipleship

hateful since it means abandoning a primary cultural value and a core social unit. Those who followed Jesus would be seen as antisocial, even, to some extent, immoral, since they didn't fulfill their obligations to their kin.

Notice that Jesus covers the gamut of our families. He begins, of course, with the deepest and longest attachment to our parents. He then moves to our nuclear family, or those that would live in the same room as we do (usually the nuclear family even slept in the same bed together, cf. Luke 11:7). Finally, he encompasses the brothers and sisters, and by extension, aunts, uncles, cousins, etc. From our deepest relationships to our more casual commitments, we abandon them in deference to Jesus. Obviously this doesn't mean we are cruel to our parents. In fact, Paul correctly orders us to care for them financially (1 Tim 5:4). Nor does it mean we cut off communication, concern, gifts, or friendships. It simply means that when a choice must be made to give deference to Jesus or our family, Jesus must win without question. "Oh, is that all it means?" Yes, and trust me, that is enough to create considerable conflict and to cast you into the class of a hateful black sheep.

Jesus gives a second requirement of discipleship. We must take up our cross and follow him (v. 27). We're no longer talking about family here, but life itself! We all know that the cross was an instrument of torture and death. Less known is the fact that the cross was so odious to the Romans that they refused to use it on their own citizens. It was reserved for the worst criminals of their conquered peoples. They particularly reveled in crucifying rebels who attempted to throw off the powerful yoke of Rome. It is in this context that Jesus makes this statement. These crowds clamor for Jesus to announce his messianic kingdom. It is their dream to once again be a free and independent state and they see Jesus as the most likely candidate to make that happen. Thus Jesus is not merely the Messiah, but a rebel leader. That, in fact,

The Preaching of Jesus

was the charge brought against him before Pilate when they said, "He claims to be king."

What Jesus is saying then is this: "You believe that I'm your king? Good, then join the revolution. But first, only come with a cross." At first this sounds quite manly—"Be willing to die before you throw down the gauntlet with me." On further reflection, however, Jesus is admitting to these would-be followers that he is a failure. He will be captured and crucified and all those who want to follow him, must be willing to join a failed revolution. Perhaps you're thinking, "That's just nuts!" If so, then you've got it. Let's be clear here. Jesus is not saying, "You must be willing to die." He's saying, "You're dead now!" He's not saying, "We'll give it our best shot and see what happens." He's saying, "We're doomed."

How is this, at any level, a reasonable proposition? Here's the secret. Jesus is so subversive that his method of winning is by abdicating the fight. By deliberately laying down his life, he would sneak up on the enemy and catch them unaware. Through death he would conquer. From our perspective we shout, "Yippee for the resurrection." That's true enough, but far too simple. You see, Jesus wasn't merely showing how *he* would win, he was calling *us* to adopt the same method. We don't merely accept Jesus' cross, we take up our own.

The cross is not merely an historical event in which we delight. It is a way of life Jesus modeled for us. To be a Christian means to imitate Jesus. To follow him is not merely to pick up the trinkets he leaves in his wake, it is to follow the arduous path he marked out for us. We are called to be subversives that win by losing, who conquer through death. We lose our egos, our financial security, even our very families to chase after this self-proclaimed loser. We do this, not because the "simple life" is much happier, not because asceticism is more peaceful. We do this because the way to victory, against all reason, is through the dark path of self-abnegation.

The Cost of Discipleship

Draw a cross on a piece of paper. On the picture, write in the names of the people, positions, and possessions you've cherished. Spend some time in prayer, asking God to deepen your understanding of and relationship with Him. Carry that cross with you in your purse or wallet.

9　　　　　　**9**

> In prayer it is better to have a heart without words than words without heart.
>
> —John Bunyon

> He who prays fervently knows not whether he prays or not, for he is not thinking of the prayer which he makes, but of God, to whom he makes it.
>
> —Francis de Sales

JESUS ON PRAYER

9　　　　　　**9**

Text: Luke 11:1-13; 18:1-14　　　　　**Memory:** Luke 11:9-13

Subtle Supernovas

In *Total Eclipse* Annie Dillard writes:

> The Ring Nebula, in the constellation Lyra, looks, through binoculars, like a smoke ring. It is a star in the process of exploding. Light from its explosion first reached the earth in 1054; it was a supernova then, and so bright it shone in the daytime. Now it is not so bright, but it is still exploding. It expands at the rate of seventy million miles a day. It is interesting to look through binoculars at something expanding seventy million miles a day. It does not budge. Its apparent size does not increase. Photographs of the Ring Nebula taken fifteen years ago seem identical to photographs of it taken yesterday.[3]

Huge happenings are not always visible to the naked eye—especially in the spiritual realm. How often it is that this nebula resembles the process of prayer. Sometimes we pray and pray and seemingly see no change in the situation. But that's only true from our perspective. If we could see from heaven's standpoint, we would know all that God is doing and intending to do in our lives. We would see God working in hearts in ways we cannot know. We would see God orchestrating circumstances that we know nothing about. We would see a galaxy of details being set in place for the moment when God brings the answer to fulfillment.

Overview of the Text Have you ever watched someone pray so fervently, so intimately, that you wondered if they actually saw God? It is an eerie experience. You walk away wishing you could talk to God like that. You begin asking questions about what experience such a spiritual master has had and what exercises have helped him/her gain such "enlightenment." Honestly, great prayer warriors make me jealous. I want what they have, but I don't know how to get it. That's precisely where the disciples were after listening to Jesus pray. One day they did something about it. They asked for a tutorial on prayer. This was not altogether uncommon. Jewish students would often ask their spiritual advisors to teach them to talk to God. Jesus, of course, was more than willing to oblige.

Pondering the Preaching of Jesus

✳ Read through these two passages on prayer and make a list of observations about prayer as well as questions you would hope to have answered about Jesus' teaching.

✳ Where did you learn how to pray? What has been most helpful in your pilgrimage into the heart of God through prayer? Where have you picked up bad habits of prayer?

Meaning of the Text   Lesson #1: *We pray "Our Father."*
This prayer is essentially the same as what we find in the Sermon on the Mount (Matt. 6:9-13). These are famous words that Jesus likely used on multiple occasions. While the whole prayer is packed with spiritual intensity, nothing is more striking than this simple two-word introduction, "Our Father." While the Jews were accustomed to thinking about Yahweh as the founder of their nation, to talk of him (or to him), as a personal, loving father was altogether new. What an outrageous thought that the creator and sustainer of the universe would be intimately concerned with our lives. To imagine the Almighty as a loving parent is nearly too much to fathom. Nevertheless, it is our contention that this is the single-most important lesson we could learn about prayer. All other lessons or exercises on prayer are merely corollaries to this overwhelming idea. If God is our father, then we pray with intensity, humility, persistence, intimacy, and obedience. The fatherhood of God changes everything pertaining to prayer. In his sermon "The Disciple's Prayer," Haddon Robinson recalls:

> When our children were small, we played a game. I'd take some coins in my fist. They'd sit on my lap and work to get my fingers open. According to the international rules of finger opening, once the finger was open, it couldn't be closed again. They would work at it, until they got the pennies in my hand. They would jump down and run away, filled with glee and delight. Just kids. Just a game. Sometimes when we come to God, we come for the pennies in his hand.
> "Lord, I need a passing grade. Help me study."
> "Lord, I need a job."
> "Lord, my mother is ill."

Jesus on Prayer

We reach for the pennies. When God grants the request, we push the hand away.

More important than the pennies in God's hand is the hand of God himself. That's what prayer is about. Perhaps the reason we don't pray well is because we've not yet comprehended the nature of him to whom we pray.

Lesson #2: *Praise should precede petition.* This second lesson comes from the overall structure of the Lord's Prayer. Before asking for daily bread or even forgiveness of sins, we are to declare the grandeur of him to whom we speak. Why? It's simple really. Until we see God on his throne, we'll not be able to adequately articulate our requests. Often praise mutates our prayers. It tends to scour off myopic requests and selfish petitions. You can't lift your eyes to God and leave your vision laying low. When we see God, we also see the world, as well as our own problems, in a different, more sanctified perspective. Shallow prayers betray a muddled vision of God's person.

Lesson #3: *Keep on asking.* Billy Graham once said, "Heaven is full of answers to prayers for which no one ever bothered to ask." This may not be the most important lesson on prayer, but it is the most oft repeated. Jesus tells two parables, constructs one poem, and draws up one metaphor, all on the same subject—persistence in prayer. The parables of the friend at midnight (Luke 11:5-8) and the persistent widow (Luke 18:1-5), are humorous tales with a very sharp point: Keep praying to God, and he will grant your requests. He chases the first parable with the brief poem, "Ask, Seek, Knock" (Luke 11:9-10). Then he pairs the parable with a metaphor of the father who gives gifts to his children (Luke 11:11-13). Simply put, Jesus persistently taught persistent prayer.

Now some will say, "Prayer doesn't actually change the mind of God but the heart of man." After all, God is sovereign and unmovable. Thus even our prayers don't move him. This is all well and good except for one small detail—*It's completely false!* This is not the place to argue about the nature of God's sovereignty. It is the place, however, to state the obvious lesson on prayer. If you keep praying, you can move the heart of God. Jesus doesn't say, "Ask and you will get what God was going to give you anyway, seek and you will find what was there all along, knock and you'll realize the door has been opened." Rather, Jesus suggests that God is like a loving father; the prayers of his children move him to action. How does this work? Who really knows? I'm not interested in the spiritual mechanics of prayer but their practical function. My prayers actually "work." Oh, I realize that requests often go unanswered, sometimes because they are selfish, misguided, or ill-timed. Nonetheless, most of us err in prayer, not because we ask with wrong motives, but because we don't ask at all.

Lesson #4: *The greatest gift to seek is the Holy Spirit.* There are many things we could ask for. In fact, Jesus said, "Whatever you ask in my name I'll give you" (cf. Matt. 18:19; 21:22; John 14:13-16; 15:7,16; 16:23-26; Eph. 3:20; 1 John 3:21). So the question is, "What things should we ask for that are in line with the will of Jesus?" That's a large and important question that will have to be answered in another essay. Suffice to say here, that the greatest gift, the most important thing we can ask for is the Holy Spirit. This is not a prayer for power. This is not a request for miraculous ability, supernatural knowledge, or a special revelation into the lottery. This is a request that the Holy Spirit would take over our lives and lead us into moral purity, evangelistic fervor, and an obedient relationship with Christ. It is painful, full of sacrifice and spiritual surgery. But it is a prayer to which Jesus will answer "Yes" every time.

Lesson #5: *Our prayers are an act of faith.* In Luke 18:8, after the parable of the unjust judge, Jesus promises that we will get justice eventually, "I tell you, he will see that they get justice, and quickly." Yes, our prayers will be answered! But he chases the promise with this question: "However, when the Son of Man comes, will he find faith on the earth?" In essence, he's asking if we will keep praying. Will we continue to believe Jesus? Will we continue to pray with confidence that he is listening? The reason our prayers are small and few is not that we lack time or self-control. The reason is that we lack faith. We simply don't believe that God is listening. Oh we might try to argue that we really *do* believe . . . at least we believe it is *possible* to answer our prayers. But if we truly thought God *would* grant our requests then certainly prayer would come more naturally and frequently.

Lesson #6: *Humility is a key to effective prayer.* Finally, the reason God answers our prayers is not that we pray well or with the right language. It is neither the multiplicity of our words nor the theological accuracy. In fact, God responds far more to our hearts than our lips. What he's looking for is worshipers who will come broken and bankrupt, with nowhere else to turn but to a loving heavenly Father. Jesus illustrates this in a story with a surprising twist (Luke 18:9-14). Everyone knows the Pharisee is trained to pray and certainly must be pretty good at it. It's equally clear that the tax collector has made a mess of his life and hasn't been in the habit of practicing religious disciplines. So who would you expect God to hear? Surprisingly, it's the guy with the black hat. Why? Because he came with a genuine need and a heart of repentance. Effective prayer is founded on a contrite heart.

Practicing the Preaching of Jesus

Take one of these lessons a day for the next six days and use them as a pivot around which your prayers revolve. Keep a journal of the kinds of things God teaches you about prayer. Note particularly which lesson(s) you have the most room to grow in.

> The real measure of our wealth is how much we'd be worth if we lost all our money.
> —John Henry Jowett

JESUS ON MONEY

Text: Matthew 19:16-30　　　　　**Memory:** Matthew 19:29-30

Money Can't Buy Happiness

In the June 14, 1968, issue of *Life* magazine appeared a picture of young David Kennedy sitting outside the White House. The picture had been taken several years before by his Aunt Jacqueline and was inscribed by his Uncle John with the words: "A future president inspects his property—John Kennedy."

Though he had name, status, wealth, and all that money could buy, in 1984 David Kennedy was found dead by his own hand at age twenty-eight.

It's been said that money will buy:
A bed, but not sleep.
Books, but not brains.
Food, but not appetite.
A house, but not a home.

Medicine, but not health.
Amusement, but not happiness.
Finery, but not beauty.
A crucifix, but not a Savior.[4]

There is a territory, a claim, a prime piece of real estate that all of us are heirs to. The Bible refers to it as "heaven." It's a city; it's a paradise; it's our home. Its cost? For some it's a bargain, a blue-light special, a once-in-a-lifetime deal that can't be passed up. For others, its price tag is too high, too lavish, too risky of a venture to bet the farm on. Read on, and you will see what we mean.

Overview of the Text

Jesus talked more about money than he did about heaven and hell. Perhaps that's because money is one of the surest ways to determine which of these places we'll wind up. It's not that money is inherently evil. In fact, in Jesus' theological culture, money was seen as a sign of God's blessing. Nor is it that monasticism is the only real way to have a relationship with Jesus. We don't rid ourselves of money because poverty is enviable but because materialism is dangerous. This story of the rich young ruler powerfully illustrates the danger of money. For him, money was a ball and chain that kept him from chasing after Jesus.

Pondering the Preaching of Jesus

✴ What is keeping you from being the fully devoted follower Jesus wants you to be? Is it money, a relationship, a job, a question, a guilty past . . . ?

✴ Do you have a biblical view of giving? What is your attitude toward the money you do give away? How quick are you to write a check to meet another's need?

✴ Tell of a time you were not financially secure and what that did to your relationship with God.

The Preaching of Jesus

Meaning of the Text

This guy is possibly the perfect convert. He is respectful, insightful, and sincere. He is young, wealthy, and influential. He is intelligent, passionate, and willing to come to Jesus. In fact, the text even goes so far as to say that Jesus loved him (Mark 10:21). He knows the Bible well and tithes his considerable resources. This is precisely the kind of young man a preacher grooms to become the chairman of the board! Jesus, however, sends him away sad, not because he lacked faith or passion but because he loved the wrong master. He just couldn't bring himself to let Jesus alone become Lord.

He came with an important question, "Teacher, what good thing must I do to get eternal life?" This is an interesting question because, in general, Jews believed they were "saved" based on God's election, *not* based on their works of righteousness. True enough, Israel's sins could send her into exile, but her salvation was based on God's good grace, not the impeccable following of the law. So he probably isn't asking how to be saved as a Jew under the Mosaic covenant but how to gain access to Jesus' new venture. He seems to be suggesting that a new kingdom is on the verge of breaking through and that Jesus is the arbiter of its entrance requirements. In short, he is asking permission to follow Jesus. He wants in on the ground floor of this new messianic movement. This young man is *really* sharp. Notice, unlike many other would-be followers, he seems to believe that this kingdom gives eternal life, not merely temporal freedom. What that might mean to him is debatable, but at least this much is certain: he has a higher view of the messianic kingdom than most are able to muster.

The master sees where the young man is headed and tries to take him even further. He asks, "Why do you call me good? None is good but God alone." Notice, Jesus is not denying that he is good, merely affirming that he is, in fact, God's envoy, enacting the incoming kingdom. In other words, God alone *is* good, and if Jesus is good, he must be acting on God's behalf. This raises the stakes of the original question, for if Jesus shares God's goodness, then he truly is capable of answering the question about how to gain eternal life.

So, the young man understands that the kingdom is at hand and that Jesus is its king. What he fails to grasp, however, is that the kingdom is about knowing Jesus, not obeying certain criterion. Entrance into the kingdom isn't through Jesus, it is *into* Jesus. This is one of those times that who you know is more important than what you do.

Jesus replies to his question in a playful way with a deadly serious edge: Keep the commandments. The young man counters, "Come on, I've been doing that all my life. . . . What do I have to do to join the club?!" "You really want to know?" Jesus replies, "Get rid of all your possessions and follow me unencumbered."

That's a problem. This young man spent the few short years of his life accumulating wealth. After all, that was seen as a sign of God's blessing. He had prospered because he worked hard, lived lawfully, and planned wisely. His money was his honor badge. It was the evidence of his righteousness before God and his validation before men. Jesus suggests, however, that a better sign of his devotion to God would be compassion to the poor. What about his validation before men? You can almost hear the wheels churning in his mind: "If I give up my money, how will everyone know how righteous I am?" (We must remember that money in his culture was not primarily used for creature comforts but to gain status.)

The young man wanted to know how to get into the kingdom. The answer was simple. Jesus must become your sole source of wealth and honor. To enter the kingdom is to come to Christ. To come to Christ requires a total resignation of all else that stands in our way, of all else in which we trust. That may be *mammon*, women, education, or any number of other noble pursuits. Jesus said it himself on another occasion, "No man can serve two masters." The cash itself was not the problem, it was his faith in the cash that was so dan-

The Preaching of Jesus

gerous. Now someone is bound to say something silly such as, "Good. If money isn't the problem, then we don't have to sell all our stuff to follow Jesus. We just need to guard against trusting in money inordinately." While that is vaguely true, we had better honestly assess whether we can hoard worldly wealth without being seduced by it. Most of us vastly overestimate our ability to live above the lure of wealth. Here we sit amidst the wealthiest nation in history, pretending that Jesus' warnings on wealth are somehow not aimed directly at us. At least this young man had the honesty to walk away sad rather than pretending Jesus wasn't talking to him. Jesus was sad for him. He really liked this one.

Turning to his own he said, "It's more difficult for a rich man to enter heaven than for a camel to pass through the eye of a needle." This was a standard idiom. The camel was the largest animal in Palestine and the eye of the needle was the smallest opening. It would be quite funny if it weren't so sad. The disciples were amazed. Who is able to live up to such unrealistically high demands? Who, then, can be saved? "Well," Jesus said, "all things are possible with God." Undoubtedly we are more comforted by this statement than Jesus intends us to be. It is *not* a magic wand to wave at Jesus' demands on wealth that will make them go away.

Peter is listening to all this and the wheels are turning. "Wait a minute. We gave up our fishing business to follow Jesus. Doesn't that count?!" "Yes it does," Jesus says, and proceeds to enumerate the incalculable riches in store for true disciples. First, the Apostles will be enthroned in heaven next to Jesus. Second, all who follow Jesus will be repaid for their sacrifice with 10,000% interest. Finally, on top of these blessings, they receive eternal life to boot.

Let's be clear here, Jesus is not calling us to be monastics but investors. True, we are to sacrifice everything to follow Jesus. In Jewish terms, Jesus calls them to leave their family and lands. That is, they must sacrifice their entire social network through the clan as well as their divine land grant in

Jesus on Money

Palestine. Nevertheless, we are not called to poverty. This side of eternity, Jesus himself is our treasure. Following him is a remarkable reward. Furthermore, our biological family will be replaced with spiritual kinship that is multiplied many times. Simply put, Jesus is a worthy reward for all that we eliminate in order to follow him. Every hindrance and obstacle must be eradicated. After grasping the pearl, they won't be missed.

We can see how family is replaced in the kingdom. But what about our land? Oh, that's the best part. There is a country to which we travel. Like Abraham, we are still on a pilgrimage. Don't be deceived or dismayed. The replacement of our family is very real—spiritual, yes, but *also* physical. Likewise, the replacement of the divine land grant is also quite physical. Normally we talk about going to heaven, but Revelation 21 tells a different story. It says, that a new heaven *and a new earth* will be created. The new Jerusalem drops from the new heaven onto the new earth and *it is there that we dwell.* So we come to this conclusion: Jesus' demand to eliminate our wealth is more real than we have heretofore assumed. Yet so is his reward. Our sacrifice of both family and land will be repaid in kind, but more spiritual, larger, and more eternal than we could have hoped.

Practicing the Preaching of Jesus

Decide today to expand the boundaries of your giving:

1) Each year, give another 2 percent of your income to your local church.
2) Empty an account, sell a home or car, and give the money to further efforts at global evangelism.
3) Adopt people in need. Find them a place to live, help them locate a job, feed them, and show them by your example that being a Christian is the best way to live.
4) Set aside all plans you have for yourself and pray. Pray that God will use you in the manner in which he wants to use you. Be obedient to His Word and His Spirit.

> The love of our neighbor is the only door out of the dungeon of self.
> —George Macdonald

> Man becomes a holy thing, a neighbor, only if we realize that he is the property of God and that Jesus Christ died for him.
> —Helmut Thielicke

THE GREAT DEBATE

Text: Matthew 22:15-46   **Memory:** Matthew 22:37-40

New Vision   One morning in 1992, as scientist Sid Nagel of the University of Chicago stood at his kitchen counter getting breakfast, something caught his attention. What he saw was a dried coffee drop on his counter. Nothing unusual about that, but what caught his eye was the way the spot had dried. Rather than having a uniform color, the coffee spot had a dark concentration of minute coffee granules at the outer edges and a much lighter color toward the middle.

To Nagel that didn't make sense. It contradicted the physics principle that says materials suspended in liquid spread randomly and as uniformly as possible.

That night Nagel discussed his observation with another professor. After suggesting some theories, he too came to the conclusion that the dried coffee spot didn't make sense. The following Friday Nagel brought the problem to a weekly bag-lunch gathering of scientists, and the mystery of the coffee spot quickly became the buzz among the university's math, computer science, chemistry, and physics faculty. For months, though, no one could solve the coffee spot mystery.

Finally a group of scientists came up with a solution that rocked the scientific community worldwide. The discovery had practical applications for paint manufacturers, electronic and computer engineers, and molecular biologists.

The ability to see the profound in the commonplace—to see a principle of physics in a coffee spot—is what makes for breakthroughs in understanding. A similar way of seeing helps us know God better. Either we can go through daily life oblivious to the activity of God around us, or we can pay attention to what God is trying to tell us in our circumstances.

Overview of the Text As tensions peak during Jesus' last week, there is this poignant encounter between the Master and the various political parties he disturbs. They come at him head on in the temple with three very difficult and premeditated questions. Their purpose is to trap him and dismantle his following. What they find, to their consternation, is that Jesus not only eludes them, he abolishes all their sophisticated arguments. In seconds, he slips their noose and hog-ties them with it. At the end of the day, Jesus alone is left standing. This illustrates how it will be when the Son of Man returns. It is indeed a dangerous thing to be found on the wrong side of this argument.

Pondering the Preaching of Jesus

- ✳ How has following Jesus changed your views of life? How has he altered your perceptions of reality?
- ✳ What difficult questions do you need answered?
- ✳ Give examples of questions people ask with ulterior motives or questions for which there really is no good answer.

The Preaching of Jesus

Meaning of the Text We must remember where we are. It is the Passover week. More specifically, it is the last week of Jesus' life. He's going out with a bang, too. On Sunday he marched down the steeps of Mount Olivet with an entourage of thousands singing his praises with a messianic chorus. This, obviously, attracted the attention of the Jewish authorities as well as the Roman peace-keeping forces. You see, to make such a march is the precursor to an inauguration. However, there was already a king in Israel named Herod who had been installed by Rome. The people apparently prefer Jesus and are willing to make the bloody sacrifice required to get him the office. I think they call this a coup.

On Monday Jesus came into the temple with a fury and did a bit of spring cleaning. That too was an overt assertion of his kingly reign soon to come. It wasn't missed by the priests nor by the Pharisees. Oh, they wanted to stop him all right. But the crowds were whipped up into a lather and rather exuberant about this new ruler. The hierarchy desperately wants to put a stop to this upstart. But they need to walk gingerly and connive shrewdly, or else they might bring their own demise rather than his.

The one advantage they have over this Galilean is their respected education. They know the Torah. They've studied logic, rhetoric, and law. These professional wordsmiths are now going to attack the master where they are the strongest. They even have home-court advantage in the temple precincts. Their attempt, clearly stated in Matthew 22:15, is to trap Jesus with a difficult question. Each of the three major political parties will come to Jesus with a particularly perplexing question. After all have tried and failed, Jesus has a question of his own. Hands down, he wins.

Strike 1 (vv. 15-22). The first to try to outwit Jesus are the Herodians. They were political collaborators with Rome, supporters of Caesar. They attempt to oust Jesus with an inquiry about taxes. Now nobody likes to pay taxes. But to pay taxes to pagan despots is particularly odious. So, one of the key requirements of a Messiah would be to liberate his people from oppressive taxation. Without economic freedom, there is no true liberation.

The question was a catch-22. If Jesus said, "No, don't pay taxes to Caesar," the Roman soldiers would jump all over him, and the Jewish leaders would have solved their problem. If, however, Jesus said, "Yes, pay taxes to Caesar," the people who chanted his name would begin to curse it. Why? Because he is no Messiah who supports Roman oppression. It seems as if Jesus just got whupped. He can say neither "nay" nor "yea." But about the time you think you've got Jesus cornered, you realize he's got you in a headlock.

Jesus calls for a coin. Someone in the crowd flips him a denarius. On the front was a picture of Tiberius Caesar, a graven image for sure. On the back were inscribed the words, "Pontif[icus] Maxim[us]" (that is, "Highest Priest"). That's a problem. No good Jew should have such a blasphemous emblem in his pocket in the first place. Why on earth would you want to keep such a thing? Hence Jesus says, "If it's got Caesar's picture on it, it must belong to him! . . . Give it back. But *you* have God's image imprinted in your spirit . . . give it to him." Suddenly all things come into strikingly clear focus. If you don't want to be ruled by Rome, stop buying into its economic system. If you claim to be led by God, then why haven't you given yourself over to him? Everyone said, "Wow," as the opposition walked away with their tails between their togas.

Strike 2 (vv. 23-33). The Sadducees step up to the plate. They were the ones who actually ran the temple and who lost the most the day before. They are going to move from politics to religion. There was one question that was particularly vexing. In fact, this was one of the key flash points between the Sadducees and the more conservative Pharisees (cf. Acts

23:6-8). For decades they had been raising the question on the resurrection. The Pharisees were, to be honest, pretty superstitious about the whole thing. For example, they believed that all Jews would be raised in Israel. However, since many were buried in Babylon, Egypt, Rome, etc., they would need to be transported to the Promised Land under-ground. Hence, the Pharisees argued that there were under-ground tunnels through which Kosher corpses rolled until arriving in Israel. It sounds quite silly. But the Sadducees were equally extreme. They were atheistic about the whole deal. They didn't believe that the dead would be resurrected at all, either as spirits, angels, or corporeally (Acts 23:8).

Knowing that Jesus is more conservative, they present him with a "worst case scenario" on resurrection. Yes, they are trying to make him look like a foolish fundamentalist. "What would happen," they ask, "if a woman went through seven brothers according to the law of levirate marriage" (cf. Deut 25:5-6)? Would this necessitate heavenly incest?

Now remember, this had been a debate which raged for decades. Even now they snicker as they wait for Jesus' answer. In one fell swoop, he decimates their ridiculous logic and articulates an incredibly powerful argument in favor of resurrection. "You're just wrong," Jesus says, "because you are ignorant of both the Bible and the power of God." (Apparently Jesus had not read *How to Win Friends and Influence People*.) Pulling a text from the Pentateuch, which the Sadducees accepted, Jesus said, "I *am* the God of Abraham, Isaac, and Jacob. . . . He is not the God of the dead but of the *living*." Notice, there are two words we have placed in italics: *am* and *living*. Many have emphasized the first word (*am*) as a key to Jesus' argument based on verb tense. That is, since God is *presently* the God of Abraham, Isaac, and Jacob, thus they must yet be alive. However, this would be a rather poor argument since God could be the God of a historic person in the past without necessitating their continued existence. Second, these men have not yet been resurrected. Oh, they

The Great Debate

are alive in spirit. But that is an entirely different argument than bodily resurrection.

I would rather suggest that the key word is not *am* but *living*. God is such a great God that he exudes life. Hence, anything that he loves, in fact, anything in his proximity, will come to life. This is not an argument merely based on verb tense, but on the very nature of God himself. Jesus snaps back at these mockers, "If you don't believe in resurrection, it is not because you are sophisticated but because your God is too small." Yahweh is life itself. Whatever he touches must, of necessity, come alive.

The Pharisees didn't want to love Jesus' answer, but they just couldn't help themselves. It was just so good.

Strike 3 (vv. 34-40). Finally, some hotshot lawyer tries to trick Jesus with a perplexing question: Which is the greatest commandment? This was not an uncommon question in Rabbinic circles. Why, with 613 commands in the Torah, and stacks of oral traditions on top of that, there were many different answers to be given, any of which might be shot through.

Jesus' reply is the same one another lawyer had given earlier in his ministry (cf. Luke 10:27). First, you love God; second, you love people. How can you argue with this? The lawyer congratulated Jesus in genuine appreciation of his insight and clarity. In return, Jesus commended him as close to the kingdom.

Homerun (vv. 41-46). Jesus surveyed the crowd with a sparkle and a glare in his eye all at the same time. No one dared ask another question. So Jesus asked one of his own. It was pretty basic really, "Why is David's son, Messiah, also called his Lord?" After all, in the Jewish social economy, the father was always greater than the son. Thus, if Messiah is David's son, how can he be called David's Lord? The text Jesus used (Ps 110:1), was a well-known verse. Hence any famous group of teachers should be able to unpack it. But it stymied them. Not only was Jesus the Messiah and David's son, he was also Immanuel, God in the flesh. As such, he is greater than David, and certainly greater than his present challengers. Thus the threat, "Until I put your enemies under your feet!" Jesus takes no guff off these guys. They were all up in his face and he slaps them back down. It is as if he says, "You better realize who it is you're messin' with."

When the Union-Pacific railroad was under construction, an elaborate trestle bridge was built over a certain large canyon in the West as part of the plan to connect St. Louis and California. Before it was open for commercial use, the construction engineer wanted to test its strength. The train was driven out to the middle of the bridge, where it was to remain for an entire day. The engineer loaded the train with extra cars and equipment to double its normal payload. One worker complained, "Are you trying to break this bridge?" "No," said the engineer. "I'm trying to prove that the bridge is unbreakable."

That's the point of this whole encounter, really. It's not about Jesus' clever repartee. It's about his extraordinary power. He's not merely a wonderful teacher. Nor can he be reduced to a charismatic political figure. He is God's Son, ruler of the kingdom. He is unbreakable. To identify him as any less is quite a dangerous thing.

Practicing the Preaching of Jesus

Ask a Christian you respect to recommend a book on the subject of Christian apologetics. Read and study the book. Make an effort in your spiritual journey to become well versed in the faith you profess belief in.

12   12

A SUBVERSIVE CRITIQUE OF RELIGION

12   12

> We can't save ourselves by pulling on our bootstraps, even when the bootstraps are made of the finest religious leather.
> —Eugene Peterson

> Better to ignore God altogether than to exploit him as a means to something else you value more highly.
> —John Boykin

> You can become a Christian by going to church just about as easily as you can become an automobile by sleeping in a garage.
> —Vance Havner

Text: Matthew 23:1-39   **Memory:** Matthew 23:11-12

Good Parenting According to the *Chicago Tribune*, a man named Joe from Rockford, Illinois, ran a live Internet sex site called Video Fantasy. Joe had a ten-year-old son. On his home computer Joe had installed filtering software to limit the surfing that his son could do on the Internet.

Joe explained, "It's not that I keep him sheltered, but my wife and I pay close attention to what he reads, what he watches on TV, and what he does on the computer because we have a responsibility to him to be the best parents we can."

Joe's sense of responsibility to his son is commendable. Joe's sense of responsibility to the children of other parents (and the parents themselves!) is at the very least, deplorable.

For many in the church today, the cancer and wildfire of hypocrisy knows no bounds.

Overview of the Text Jesus has a reputation for being a nice guy. That's really not quite true. He could be rather ruthless. Here, in fact, he's about as mean as he gets. Face to face with the Pharisees, he critiques their religion and feathers fly. Clearly this is a fascinating encounter . . . fights usually are. But Matthew doesn't record it merely because it's interesting. He records it because it is autobiographical for the church. All too often we wind up looking like these guys and loving the same things they cherished. That's why this chapter is so deeply troubling and so desperately needed. It has never been more contemporary than today.

Pondering the Preaching of Jesus

✗ As you read through Matthew 23:1-39, make a list of grievances Jesus had against the Pharisees.

✗ In a moment of personal evaluation, what are you doing outside the walls of the church that is hypocritical and may be a hindrance to an unbelieving onlooker?

✗ What religious "ritual" in your church needs to be addressed? Without changing the message, what methods for reaching people or "doing church" need to be evaluated?

Meaning of the Text Let's get one thing straight right up front. The Pharisees were not demonic. The truth of the matter is they were religious men with a passion for the Bible. They squabbled over correct doctrine. They worked *hard* to help people know what God had said. They were vigilant in synagogue attendance, tithing, prayers, and Bible study. Because of their concerted effort in religious affairs, they were deeply respected in their communities.

So why does the Bible speak so viciously against them if they were the suit-and-tie guys in church? There was just one

A Subversive Critique of Religion

little problem they had. It can be called *the sin of self*. They were more interested in self-promotion than the heart of God. It was not that they didn't care about God or his law—that would be utterly false. But their concern for self blinded them to the real heart of God. It so led them astray that Jesus had his most intense disagreements with them and reserved his harshest criticism for them.

Jesus begins by recognizing just what we've said above. Namely, these men were right in their interpretation of the Mosaic law and had the authority to speak the truth. Therefore, one was wise to follow their words. Their walk, on the other hand, would lead you down a treacherous spiritual path. Their demand for titles and self-promotions knew no bounds. Now, this is really not so different with many religious leaders today . . . or politicians, lawyers, college professors, preachers, athletes, or housewives. It seems so natural, in fact, that some may doubt the serious nature of the sin of self. Perhaps we'd better look closely at its consequences.

There are seven WOES between vv. 13 & 32. The first six come in matching pairs. The last one is the *coup de grâce*. While this may appear, at first, as a harangue of miscellaneous grievances, on closer inspection, a refined outline surfaces.

Woes #1-2 (vv. 13-15), *Evangelizing people into hell.* The Pharisees were quite evangelistic. It wasn't so much that they brought people into Judaism in order to know God. Rather, when someone did convert, they would snatch him or her into their own particular brand of pharisaic observance. They would inflame them with a passion for divisive and legalistic doctrine. Yet their narrow observance missed the heart of God. So once a person showed an interest in God, they were distracted by the Pharisees into a passion for religion, which obscured a relationship with God. Their satisfaction shifted from knowing their creator to following man-made rules. Ritual replaced real spirituality. It is simply heinous in God's eyes, particularly since Jesus was the object of their rejection.

The Preaching of Jesus

It is at this point that Jesus calls them *hypocrites*. Now that's truly funny. You see, there was no functional equivalent in the Hebrew (or Aramaic) language for the word *hypocrite*. Why? Well, because it was a term that came out of Greek theater, the very theater Kosher Jews refused to attend. It indicated an actor who wore a mask. They were hiding their true identity on stage and playing the part of another. Why is that so funny? Well, because Jesus was calling the Pharisees "play actors" from a theater that they wouldn't even attend! That won't go over so well . . . but it is still pretty funny.

Woes # 3-4 (vv. 16-24), *Oppressing people through religious ritual*. There were two rituals in particular that Jesus attacked. He could have targeted more, to be sure, but *oaths* and *tithes* were enough to prove his point. He objected to pharisaic oaths because they were nothing more than legal fine print. They had this "rule" that an oath is only valid if collateral could be collected on it. Hence, if one swore by the temple, there was no way you could make him pay, since he couldn't very well hand you the deed to the temple. However, if he swore by the gold of the temple that was a different story. After all, he could purchase, replace, or otherwise own the gold of the temple (even though it might take a Herculean effort). Or again, if someone swore by the altar, it was not valid collateral. However, the carcass on the altar could be obtained. The upshot is that they used a religious ritual to purposely defraud people. How wrong is that?! Jesus dealt with this very issue a couple of years earlier in the Sermon on the Mount (5:33-37). There he concluded, "Simply let your 'yes' be 'yes' and your 'no,' 'no.'"

The second ritual Jesus assailed was tithes. Oh, there was nothing actually wrong with their tithe, per se. What Jesus objects to is that one could be so cautious to give God garden herbs but give no consideration to those God loves. How can one spend so much time and attention at church (and its satellite activities) and ignore compassion for the

A Subversive Critique of Religion

Father's wounded children? But ritual is often like that. We think that by carrying out religious duties we become special to God. The truth is, however, that religious ritual is usually not what we do for God but gifts he offers us—church, Bible reading, baptism, communion, worship, etc. So we open God's presents and pretend we are fulfilling some divine obligation in so doing. What's worse is that we have neglected our true duties to God (i.e., compassion and mercy), under the illusion that we have fulfilled them merely by receiving God's gifts!

Woes #5 & 6 (vv. 25-28), *Their purity was only external.* It's been said that beauty is skin deep, but ugly goes clean to the bone. That is certainly true in this instance. Jesus compares the Pharisees to dirty dishes and tombstones. Now that would raise a few eyebrows, not to mention a good bit of "dander." These guys prided themselves on ritual purity. To accuse them of being disingenuous . . . well, them's fightin' words. It hardly needs to be said that dead men's bones were considered highly defiling in the Jewish economy. Each year before the pilgrims came to the feasts in Jerusalem, the locals painted the tombs lest someone inadvertently step on one and become defiled. Jesus accuses them of being those whitewashed tombs. They look good on the outside, but inside they are full of defilement. Anyone who gets near them will be unclean.

When Howard Carter and his associates found the tomb of King Tutankhamen, they opened up his casket and found another within it. They opened up the second, which was covered with gold leaf, and found a third. Inside the third casket was a fourth made of pure gold. The pharaoh's body was in the fourth, wrapped in gold cloth with a gold mask. But when the body was unwrapped, it was leathery and shriveled.

Whether we are trying to cloak a dead spiritual life, or something else, in caskets of gold to impress others, the beauty of the exterior does not change the absence of life on the interior. And though the text doesn't tell us the reaction of the Pharisees, it could surely have been measured with both a barometer and a thermometer.

Woe #7 (vv. 29-39), *They kill prophets.* Jesus accuses them of murdering the prophets. Now, obviously, they weren't even alive at the time. Nonetheless, a son adopted the posture (and often even the guilt), of his forefathers. Thus, Jesus is simply saying, "Like father, like son." They deny it. Their evidence is all the mausoleums they erected in the prophets' honor. Jesus says, "Yeah, yeah, I see all those. But I also see your hearts and what you are about to do to me." Because Jesus was the culmination of all prophetic preaching, what they do to him would epitomize and magnify what was done to all the other prophets. Of course, this was the very kind of bodacious claim that kept getting Jesus in trouble in the first place. Now the Pharisees are not just insulted, but are all up in a huff about this blasphemous claim. Yet they could hardly deny the piercing truth of Jesus' words. They did have a plot afoot to take his life. They couldn't deny that their fathers had stoned, flogged, rejected, and killed Jesus' prophetic predecessors. Nor could they deny their own machinations to do the same to him. Laid bare before the public, they bristle at Jesus' accusations and redouble their efforts to kill him.

Let's come full circle here. We began by suggesting that the sin of self was the culprit behind all these other faults. And it is. We also suggested that Christians today often look more like the Pharisees than they do Jesus. And we do. But could it also be true that our ultimate offense is in rejecting Jesus? "Oh no, we honor Jesus by going to church, reading the Bible, tithing, etc." Don't you see? That is exactly the defense the Pharisees gave. If it quacks like a duck, walks like a duck, and swims like a duck . . . it's probably a duck. If we talk like a Pharisee, act like a Pharisee, and promote ourselves like Pharisees, guess what? Our relationship with Jesus will be no different than the Pharisees'. Look deeply in this text. It demands introspection.

A Subversive Critique of Religion

Set aside 5 minutes at the end of every day for 1 week and evaluate your day. Think about the false impressions you gave during that day. Think about the lies that were told. Think about areas of weakness in your spiritual life that you are covering up and not addressing. Spend time at the end of each evaluation repenting before God. Ask God to help you tear away the coverings and false fronts. Ask God to help you deal with insecurities, with the guilt and shame that only the two of you know about. Ask God to help you be an authentic follower.

THE END IN SIGHT

> The best way to prepare for the coming of Christ is never to forget the presence of Christ.
> —William Barclay

> I wish I could be alive when Christ returns because I would like to be the first earthly monarch to take my crown and lay it at his feet.
> —Queen Elizabeth the First of England

> We are not a postwar generation, but a pre-peace generation. Jesus is coming.
> —Corrie ten Boom

Text: Matthew 24:1–25:46   **Memory:** Matthew 25:34-36

The Shout Missionary Gregory Fisher recounts a surprising question one of his West African Bible college students asked him. Citing 1 Thessalonians 4:16, the student asked what the Lord would shout when he descended from heaven with a loud command.

I wanted to leave the question unanswered, to tell him that we must not go past what Scripture has revealed, but my mind wandered to an encounter I had earlier in the day with a refugee from the Liberian civil war.

The man, a high school principal, told me how he was apprehended by a two-man death squad. After several hours of terror, . . . he narrowly escaped. After hiding in the bush for two days, he was able to find his family and escape to a neighboring country. The escape cost him dearly: two of his children lost their lives. The stark cruelty unleashed on an unsuspecting, undeserving population had touched me deeply.

I also saw flashbacks of the beggars that I pass each morning on my way to the office. . . . I am haunted by the vacant eyes of people who have lost all hope.

. . . The question hadn't gone away. "'Enough,'" I said "He will shout, 'Enough!' when he returns."

. . . "Enough suffering. Enough starvation. Enough terror. Enough death. Enough indignity. Enough lives trapped in hopelessness. Enough sickness and disease. Enough time. Enough!"[5]

Overview of the Text

Matthew 24 is one of the most debated passages in the Bible. Here Jesus describes two events—the destruction of the temple in Jerusalem and his return. The problem is that he doesn't clearly differentiate between the two. Therefore, it's difficult for us to know which words apply to A.D. 70 and which words are yet to be fulfilled at his return. So theologians bicker about where to draw the line in the text between past and future. As a result, folks assume that they can't understand Jesus' overall message because scholars can't agree on details. Indeed, the details are difficult to decipher. The overarching message, however, is obvious and essential. Differ with the details if you must, but at least discern this much: In spite of great tribulation, Jesus *will* return and bring about justice. And when he does, you'd better be ready.

Pondering the Preaching of Jesus

✳ Photocopy Matthew 24. Underline verses that seem to speak primarily about the destruction of Jerusalem. Circle verses that seem to speak primarily about Jesus' return. Highlight with a marker verses that could comfortably go either way.

✳ If you knew Jesus was coming today, what would you do to get ready?

✳ What excites you most about heaven?

The Preaching of Jesus

Meaning of the Text The disciples are duly impressed with the massive buildings of the temple. After all, the nation had been working on it for five decades and it was something to behold. The Apostles aren't just gawking at it, however, they are making dibs for office space. They are convinced that they will soon rule from the temple with Jesus as their king. Their mistaken perception was not without a realistic foundation. Just that week Jesus had marched into Jerusalem on a donkey in a triumphal procession, cleansed the temple, and silenced all opposition in the temple debates. The boys have reason to believe that this was the big one.

When they asked Jesus if he noticed how big the buildings were, he said, "Yeah, but they'll soon be leveled." Then he turned on his heels and walked off! About ⅗ of a mile later they catch up with him on the western slope of the Mount of Olives. They begin to grill him about it. Jesus launches into a long discourse about the destruction of Jerusalem as well as his Second Coming. He makes a number of important points.

There will be warning signs (vv. 4-14). Jesus calls these signs birth pangs. In other words, they aren't the real deal, only preliminary signs leading up to it. He says there will be things like wars, famines, earthquakes, and false messiahs. At first we sit up and listen attentively saying, "Okay, so if I know when these things come, then I'll know when Jesus will return." After thinking about it, however, we say, "Wait a minute, these sorts of things *always* take place." Jesus is not giving us an hourglass that will count down to his coming. Rather, he is painting a picture of what it will be like so that we can be prepared to hunker down through difficult times until he does come. In other words, this advice is for preparation, not for prediction. They direct us how to live; they don't tell us when the end will come. Furthermore, each of these signs would as easily apply to A.D. 70 as to the Second Coming. So they really tell us nothing but "be ready for troubling times."

The End in Sight

When you see trouble, run! (vv. 15-25). A terrible event is looming over the horizon. It is called the "Abomination of Desolation." This has something to do with the destruction of the temple in an especially sacrilegious way. When will that take place? Well, it already has . . . three times. The first time this prophecy from Daniel 9:27 was fulfilled was when the evil Syrian king, Antiochus Epiphanes, sacrificed a pig on the altar in 168 B.C. It was just awful. Priests were killed, women were raped, and the temple was ransacked. The second time was in 63 B.C. when the Roman ruler, Pompey, marched his armies into the capital city to break up a civil war among the Jews. He went so far as to enter the Holy of Holies. The historical records say he found it empty. The third time was, of course, A.D. 70 when the Roman armies finally broke through the barricades of the city to squelch the rebellion against Caesar. Jesus' advice was to flee the city when they saw the Romans encircling it (cf. Luke 21:20). This was excellent, although counterintuitive advice. The natural response of the ancient village was to run to the walled city when attacked. However, if the walls fall, you're in deep trouble. Jesus knew the city would be punished, thus he advised his followers to get out while the gettin' was good. In fact, their window of opportunity was so small that they needed to escape without even packing a bag. And they'd better hope this seizure doesn't take place in winter or on a Sabbath for that would make their flight all the more difficult. History tells us that the Christians did, in fact, escape, heeding Jesus' advice. Consequently, they were spared the gruesome fate that befell their fellow Jews in A.D. 70.

Cataclysmic events (vv. 26-31). During these events, there will be galactic signs. The Son of Man will appear all over the sky like lightning. Stars will fall and the sun won't shine (an apocalyptic image that describes the fall of great nations). Angels will scour the earth for the elect. This is downright weird stuff. And why shouldn't it be? These words are primarily describing future, eschatological events that are beyond

The Preaching of Jesus

    When will all this take place? Well, verses 32 and 36 dis-
cuss that. On the one hand, certain events will take place
within that generation (v. 34) that will be recognizable. In
other words, there were some things that Christians could
discern concerning Jerusalem's demise. The rising political
tensions, the famine as a result of Roman encampment, the
civil unrest among the Jews themselves, all these are harbin-
gers of a coming catastrophe. Simply put, there was some
handwriting on the wall that was as easy to read as a fig
tree's budding leaves.

    On the other hand, there are some events that we can-
not predict. In fact, Jesus himself was unable to predict them.
(Those today who claim they can, have an overinflated view
of their abilities . . . not to mention an interesting ethic of selling for profit books which predict the imminent end of the
age.) We have tended to make Jesus omniscient.
Incarnationally he was not. In fact, he claims not to have
known when he would return. This is, perhaps, why he
doesn't differentiate between 70 A.D. and the *parousia*,
because he, himself, was not sure about the details. Be that
as it may, all he can tell us is that the coming of the Romans
would be pretty obvious, yet *his* coming was mysterious.

    Six Parables on the Parousia (24:37-25:46). This collection
of parables is like a diamond. It has a singular point (which is
quite stunningly beautiful). Yet each parable adds an angle
that reflects the light with a different hue. (1) Jesus' return will
be like Noah and the Ark (24:37-41). In spite of persistent
warnings, people didn't discern the times. They continued to
live life normally and were overwhelmed suddenly with a
judgment. *Jesus will come when people don't expect it.* Therefore,
we'd better be ready. (2) Thieves don't announce their itiner-
ary (24:42-44). *Likewise, Jesus will come unexpectedly.* Therefore,
we'd better be ready. (3) When the master goes away, he

The End in Sight

88 assigns stewards to care for his affairs (24:45-51). The longer he's gone, the more it feels like he will never return. The fact is, the longer he's gone, the more imminent his return. Therefore, the wise steward is constantly attentive to his duties. *Jesus could come sooner than you think.* Therefore, we'd better be ready. (4) The maidens at a wedding are responsible for the reception at the groom's house when he brings home his bride (25:1-13). The foolish neglect to make appropriate provisions. So when he's delayed, the dimwits are stuck outside with dim wicks. *Jesus may come later than expected.* Therefore, we'd better be ready. (5) When employers leave, they entrust their assets to middle management, and they expect a return on their investment when they return. Those with a good profit are duly rewarded. Those who banked on the guy going bankrupt will be sorely surprised at how ruthless he can be. *Likewise, when Jesus returns, he will expect to find us faithful.* Therefore, we'd better be ready. (6) This last parable is really more of a metaphor. That is, it's a real picture, only its painted with apocalyptic imagery. There's no fiction here. *The hard reality is that Jesus will wield his authority as judge when he returns.* Therefore, we'd better be ready.

In case you've not caught it yet, there is a recurring theme to this chapter. Jesus did not give us this information to titillate our curiosity about end-time events. He is screaming for our attention! If he doesn't get it, there'll be hell to pay.

Practicing the Preaching of Jesus

Make a list of all the people you are excited about seeing again in heaven as well as all the people you are eager to meet for the first time. Make a list of all the people you know are not headed in that direction who need help finding their way.

1. Cited by Craig Brian Larson in *Illustrations for Preaching & Teaching* (Grand Rapids: Baker, 1993), p. 125.

2. Excerpted from *No Wonder They Call Him the Savior* © 1986 by Max Lucado (Sisters, OR: Multnomah, 1986), pp. 157-159. Used by permission of Multnomah Publishers, Inc.

3. Annie Dillard, *Total Eclipse* (New York: HarperCollins, 1994).

4. Received via e-mail, original source unknown.

5. Gregory Fisher, *Illustrations for Preaching & Teaching,* ed. by Craig Brian Larson (Grand Rapids: Baker, 1993), pp. 210-211.

About the Authors

Mark Moore is Professor of New Testament at Ozark Christian College, teaching in the areas of Life of Christ, Acts, and Bible Interpretation. Mark did his undergraduate work at Ozark Christian College. He went on to earn a Masters in Education from Incarnate Word College in San Antonio, Texas, while pastoring a bilingual church there. Later he earned a Masters in Religious Studies from Southwest Missouri State University. He returned to Ozark to teach in the fall of 1990.

Mark is the author of a number of books, including other works on the Life of Christ: a two-volume set entitled *The Chronological Life of Christ*, and the more devotional *Encounters with Christ*. He is a popular speaker for both adult and youth conferences.

Mark makes his home in Joplin, Missouri, where his favorite place is with his wife, Barbara, and two teenage children, Josh and Megan, who both know and honor the Lord.

Jon Weece is currently ministering with Southland Christian Church in Lexington, Kentucky. He began in the summer of 2000 on the Teaching Team and as an Adult Discipleship Associate. Jon has served four years as a missionary in Haiti.

He graduated with a Bachelor of Biblical Literature degree from Ozark Christian College in Joplin, Missouri. He and his wife Allison live in Lexington. Jon is passionate about being a good husband and dad. He also enjoys a good Sunday afternoon drive, cooking steaks on the grill, reading a good book, and fishing.

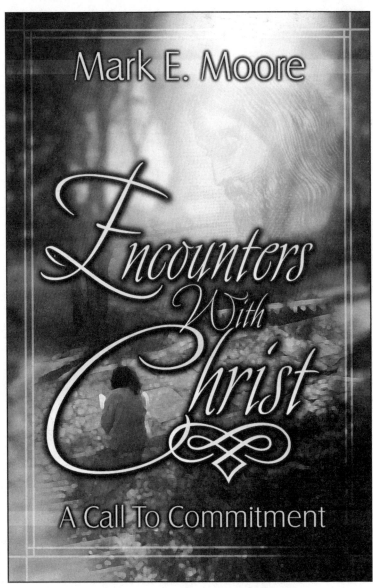

HOW TO
DODGE
A
DRAGON

A DEVOTIONAL

READING

OF REVELATION

Mark E. Moore